WITHDRAWN

The Drift of Western Thought

The Drift
of Western Thought

By

CARL F. H. HENRY, TH.D., PH.D.,

Professor of Systematic Theology and Christian Philosophy
Fuller Theological Seminary

The W. B. Riley Memorial Lectures
Northwestern Schools

1951

WM. B. EERDMANS PUBLISHING COMPANY
Grand Rapids 1951 **Michigan**

Introduction

The world is aflame with crisis, and the end is not yet.

Not all the sleepy-eyed prophets of unlimited progress are disillusioned by the failure of their grandiose dreams. Some keep up their familiar chant: day by day the world gets better and better, in some mysterious way — if no longer in every way, as they were once prone to say.

But the Bible brings before us the awesome perspective of eternity; it confronts us with God's view of man and the world. In its message, proclaimed by spokesmen for the holy and merciful Lord, can be found the only escape from the modern cultural debacle. Back to the God who has revealed Himself, away from the idols of modern men — that is our lone hope.

This ability of the Christ of the Bible to lift our age out of the shambles of paganism runs through this series of lectures as a constant note. Penetrating and persuasive, these lectures will long be recalled by the thousands who heard them in person and by radio, as a sober and scholarly presentation of the only cure for an otherwise fatal sickness of our era. They hold an interest that is not confined to the collegian and seminarian at Northwestern Schools, where they constituted the 1951 W. B. Riley Memorial Lectures, for they deal with a universal predicament and with a remedy that reaches far as the curse is found. Men of Christian conviction will be strengthened in faith, and those of contrary conviction will be called to account, by the pages of this timely and able volume.

BILLY GRAHAM

Contents

THE
PARTITIONS OF WESTERN THOUGHT:
ANCIENT AND MEDIEVAL

I

The Partitions of Western Thought:
Ancient and Medieval

WHEN Hitler's storm troops jabbed like lightning
across the scarred face of Europe, intending to carve
a mid-century contour modeled by *Mein Kampf,* a brilliant
philosopher was reminding us graduate students that even
a dictator who could smash through the rugged Maginot
Line would find it immeasurably harder to cancel out the
distinctions elaborated in the history of philosophy.

The "durable divides" are ideological, not geographical.
So we learned with vigor from Professor W. Harry Jellema,
who stalked around his Indiana classroom with one eye on
the movements of Hitler and Stalin and the other on the
movements of thought. History is divided, he reminded us,
into three distinct periods — ancient, medieval and modern
— for stubborn philosophical reasons. Not by military vic-
tories or defeats, but by the rise and fall of diverse intellectual temperaments those partitions were erected; the
ancient mind, the medieval mind, the modern mind stand
apart through a warfare of the intellect more than through
force of muscle and sword. Each epoch is distinguished
from the others by a diverse way of discerning facts and of
assessing their importance. Peculiar to each is a genius, a
certain homogeneity of outlook, which requires a distinction
between them. And the struggle of our moment, in the

arena of world affairs, is not intelligible apart from this larger conflict of ideologies, whose broad outlines are exhibited to us in the great speculative divides of the history of ideas.

Few eras have been drilled as meticulously in the stark contrast of ideologies as our own mid-twentieth century. Individuals now feel constrained, as never in our lifetime, to range themselves on determinate sides, whether in the classroom, in the workshop or office, at the market or at home. Warier than ever of entangling alliances, men's loyalties are not easily changed. Sober discussion of the meaning and destiny of life, which had all but evaporated from the American scene, has been thrust again to the fore by the dire outlook of our times, so that the contemporary man is more and more primed for debate on ultimate issues.

The attempt to penetrate the logical basis of modern culture, in contrast with the rationale of the ancient and medieval epochs, has issued in multiplied confusion. H. G. Wells wrote, before his death, of *Mind at the End of Its Tether*. The whole frame of reference within which modern man seeks the meaning of life and the solution of his persistent problems displays its inadequacy in test after test. No era so replete with inner tension, so empty of synthesis, is found in the history of philosophy, except perhaps for the years 200-100 B. C. Every conceivable merger of propositions is consummated in the matrimonial mart of modern thought. This shuffling of ideas, as if they were but cards in a game of chance, increases the common inquiry whether, after all, we ought to be asking not what meaning life has, but whether it has meaning at all. Pre-war optimism gone, temporal security imperiled, old cliches outmoded, the modern man — finding no logical basis of things — is tempted to think that all genuine promise of integration is gone, and with it the hope of outwitting despair.

Such indecision cannot but leave its scars upon history in our day. Just as in ancient times, the loss of confidence in classic idealism and the collapse of Graeco-Roman culture pockmarked temple and home alike, so, too, today the crumbling of the prevailing philosophic structure sooner or later will affect the destiny of all whom it involves. Dismantle the framework within which men make their decisive choices and some wreckage in all the areas of life is inescapable. It is no inconsequential matter to unmask the accepted pattern of meaning as inadequate to explain the course of human experiences and world events. The breakdown of a culture means the frustration of a people; the lengthened shadows of cultural collapse serve as bridges from bafflement to nihilism.

The lone escape from despair and meaninglessness is a satisfying rationale, one which will make meaningful also the very ruin of the culture of the moment. For if there be hope, there had better be a reason for it. Interestingly enough, the modern world-life view is one which, we can be sure, neither the best ancient nor medieval minds would have applauded. Whatever differences may separate Plato and Aristotle from Augustine and Aquinas, and each from the others, they would all have resisted the modern rationale as involving, quite necessarily, an eventual collapse. Their astonishment doubtless would have been the modern surprise that the cultural enterprise has come to such a demise. For nothing is more certainly gleaned from a study of their first principles than that a framework with the modern restrictions could not long retain significance for history and man. They could have seen *The Crisis of Our*

Age, as Pitirim A. Sorokin aptly titled his book, from afar off. The modern outlook would have been seen as involving its own undoing, as not being what it professed to be, a logical basis for any cultural enterprise.

Precisely this suggestion that there are *kinds of rationale,* each based in different ways on the assumption that reality is somehow intelligible and interpretable in terms of mind, is instructive. For it indicates how profitable it may be to survey those contrastive frames of reference which distinguish the ancient, the medieval and the modern outlooks, in the firm hope that we there shall find signs of warning and of encouragement in the dark night to which western culture has come.

1. The Ancient Mind

Classic philosophy, the loftiest scaffolding for Graeco-Roman culture, was unambiguously idealistic. To the supernatural realm, the ancient mind in this influential expression assigned logical priority. Only in relation to an eternal, purposive, spiritual sphere are nature and man meaningful. Man is qualitatively superior to the animals because of this rational link to the supernatural; he is not merely a creature of time and space. Moral distinctions are objective and eternal, not merely relative and arbitrary.

These great affirmations are at the heart of Socratic-Platonic-Aristotelian philosophy. From our viewpoint these convictions are the most important achievement of the ancient mind, which might well, in evaluating its significance, be prized for its idealistic rebuttal of naturalism. They overshadowed the disagreements on which the philosophic genius of antiquity divided. On these issues not only were Socrates, Plato and Aristotle a unity, but even successors who repudiated the Platonic-Aristotelian synthesis were unable to avoid their influence, as for example the Stoics, whose inconsistencies derive in many cases from an inability to free themselves from Aristotelian emphases.

This idealistic frame was consciously opposed to the naturalistic school which in Greek antiquity had come to its most systematic expression in Democritus. The classic philosophers realized that if Democritus remained unchallenged, Greek culture was doomed. The warning that culture is on the brink of destruction is so much a modern motif that the classic struggle against ancient naturalism immediately enlists our interest. Why was Democritus' naturalistic interpretation of the movement of things fraught with such peril for man and history? Were the idealists right?

Democritus, the laughing philosopher, wanted a thoroughgoing materialism: nature is the ultimate real; the system of atoms in motion is the only underlying reality. All existence he explains simply in terms of this combination and recombination of atoms, determined by an all-embracing necessity. Both gods and men alike are referred to nature as their cause, and not nature and life to a supernatural origination. Mind is not distinguished essentially from matter; rather, the material arrangement resulting in mental activity involves only the motion of smoother, finer and more agile atoms than those operating in non-mental phenomena. The gods are explained likewise; deities are made of more refined particles, hence their atoms do not wear out as quickly as the rest of nature — they attain longevity, but not eternity, for nature bows to time. Clearly enough, Democritus applied the materialistic philosophy with as much zest and thoroughness as many a contemporary naturalist, even if his formulation appears rather crude and unrefined in contrast with the artistic and literary expression with which the theory is frequently embellished in modern times.

The idealists discerned that Democritean and Sophistic philosophy offered no basis for a durable Greek culture. They were concerned with Sophism even more than with Democritus, for it involved all of reality in flux. A universe in which everything changes is an unintelligible universe; in that sort of a universe, they insisted, even philosophers should maintain the silence of vegetables.

Democritus no less than the Sophists had evaporated the meaning of the whole course of events; furthermore, he had robbed human life and nature of purpose. Explain men and things wholly in terms of efficient causation, account for effects by the mere reference to whatever causes immediately precede them, and one critically banishes the realm of ends, or final causes, for the sake of which all things exist. Description in terms solely of efficient causation might suffice for some situations (Plato and Aristotle would not object to being overheard by the modern scientist) but such explanation really involves an abstraction, and becomes unjustifiable dogmatism when represented as complete. The universe can be understood only teleologically; a world without meaning and purpose makes no room even for Democritus writing a book and expecting that his readers will understand him. Reality viewed as unthinking process sacrifices morality as well as truth; man is reduced to an animal, however much shrewder than other beasts he might be. That sort of a universe is a meaningless universe, a worthless and purposeless universe; it becomes necessary to forfeit the significance of everything, human existence and thinking included.

The Greek idealists did not present their supernaturalistic rationale of things, however, simply as arbitrary dogma. With a life-or-death earnestness, they entered the philosophic arena convinced that the case for a teleological idealism could be rationally proved, and that the naturalistic alternative rested on insufficient reason. The divine-human dialectic involved in the search for truth was already a concern of Socratic philosophy, which did not confine its interest to the natural realm. Plato and Aristotle stressed the reality and priority of the supernatural, the qualitative uniqueness of man, and the objectivity of morals with such earnestness that they left to later generations an entire philosophical library centering in the classic framework; from each has come, in extant writings alone, a collection which even in modern times would appear a most prodigious achievement by a single thinker.

To what extent ancient idealism and Graeco-Roman culture mixed is a matter of debate. Gibbon, in his history of the Roman empire, placed the cultural collapse late, and regarded the second century of our era as a sort of golden age; Toynbee, the contemporary philosopher of history, dates the breakdown of Greek culture as early as the Peloponnesian war, and Spengler holds that the great philosophers always appear toward the end of an era, as a sign that deterioration is well on its way. In any event, whatever Greek and Roman multitudes may have been enlisted by classic idealism, as the alternative to naturalism, the witness of history is all too evident that the higher philosophy did not furnish a dynamic that precluded the collapse of ancient culture. There is something to be said for the view that a considerable loyalty to the idealistic tradition was won for a time by the Platonic-Aristotelian movement, with reflections in the various areas of cultural interprise, both the arts and the sciences. Greek culture had influential expressions, in varying degrees, of the idealistic view of things. Naturalism remained throughout the ancient era a submerged and uninfluential option precisely because the response of the masses, in terms of Greek idealism, established that framework as classical, or highest in order of merit. That the primordial reality is spirit sweeps like a fire of assurance through the ancient thought of Plato and Aristotle, and characterizes later Neo-Platonism. The ancient mind was convinced in its idealistic expositions that concentration on atoms rather than on the supernatural could only mean the doom of everything worthwhile. Whether in government or sculpture, in literature or art, Greek culture, in major manifestations, patterned itself around the convictions that man is uniquely related to a supernatural realm of abiding goodness, truth and beauty. Greek customs and institutions, political, social, and religious, aimed to realize more fully that supernatural ideal which the classic philosophers found implicitly embodied in the actual structure of things, and which was uncovered to philosophic contemplation.[1]

The breakdown of Greek culture, as a phenomenon of history, is a commonplace in every student's kit of knowledge. The classic synthesis forged around the notion of cultural *harmony,* or *the mean,* fell apart under both internal

1. W. R. Inge has expressed well that the object of Greek philosophy was "to teach man to live well, and with that object to think rightly about God, the world, and himself. This close union between metaphysics, morals, and religion has remained as a permanent possession of the modern world. Every philosopher is now expected to show the bearing of his system on morality and religion, and the criticism is often justified that however bold the speculations of the thinker, he is careful, when he comes to conduct, to be conventional enough" (in R. W. Livingstone, ed., *The Legacy of Greece,* 45, Oxford: Clarendon Press, 1921).

and external pressure. Despite the concentration upon the supernatural and the objectivity of the moral claim, the ethical fibre of Greek culture was unable to resist deterioration. Ancient culture lacked power, power to achieve moral standards which — although sub-Christian by a later contrast — were idealistic and supra-naturalistic. If the Greek city-states failed politically to work out the ideal harmony between the various states, and between the states and the individual, and issued already in the Greek breakdown of 404 B. C.,[2] still further setbacks were to be recorded, despite classical philosophy, in 330 B. C. and 410 A. D.

Between Aristotle and Neo-Platonism stood, as the most influential philosophies, Epicureanism and Stoicism; neither movement made room for the supernatural, nor for a moral order to be distinguished from the necessity of nature. The monotheistic bent of the idealistic philosophies had already weakened the popular polytheistic religion. Consequently, many who had fragmentarily appropriated the classic view, were quite ready to welcome less demanding moral philosophies. Epicurus set his moral theory in the context of Democritean materialism, whereas Stoicism, while it retained the classic teleology, was also a thoroughly deterministic nature-

2. G. Lowes Dickinson commented that "this harmony which was the dominant feature in the consciousness of the Greeks and the distinguishing characteristic of their epoch in the history of the world, was nevertheless, after all, but a transitory and imperfect attempt to reconcile elements whose antagonism was too strong for the solution thus proposed. The factors of disruption were present from the beginning in the Greek ideal; and it was as much by the development of its own internal contradictions as by the invasion of forces from without that that fabric of magical beauty was destined to fall" (*The Greek View of Life*, 231. New York: McClure, Phillips & Co., 1906, 5th ed.).

philosophy.[3] The significance of personal decision was reduced in Stoicism, to enthusiastic resignation to one's environment. The sting was removed from such resignation by pantheism: the deterministic necessity of nature was also a divine necessity, worthy of worship. Here the distinction was blurred between the actual and the ideal; the *ought* was nothing more or less than the *is*.

The welcome given Stoicism sets in clear relief the cardinal weaknesses of the classic philosophy. Too simple a view of human nature, however much more profound it was than that of naturalism, stood at the center of Greek idealism. On one side, the Platonic-Aristotelian emphasis on man's rational relation to the supernatural was developed so as to minimize any disparity between man and God except in terms of man's incompleteness. The classic man could be, on the psychic side, fitted quite comfortably into a pantheistic scheme of things; that stress on sin which, in Hebrew theology, accented man's separation from God not merely in terms of creaturehood, but also in terms of conscious moral revolt, was absent. On the other side, the classic emphasis on the reality and priority of the supernatural created as many problems as it 'solved, for the philosophers were less explicit about the religious aspect of their views

---

3. Albert Schweitzer wrote: "One watches with dismay the shaping of the fate of ancient ethics in Epicureanism and Stoicism. In place of the vigorous life-affirming ethic which Socrates expects from rational thinking, resignation steps in. An inconceivable impoverishment takes place in the representation of the moral. The notion of action cannot be worked out to completion" (*The Philosophy of Civilization*, 120. New York: The Macmillan Company, 1949).

than the thirst of the human spirit requires.[4] The Platonic-Aristotelian deity did not even enter into the world of change. The divinely significant was not to be found in time, but rather in the supra-temporal.[5] The value of prayer was unclear; contemplation was the philosophic supreme good. Immortality was an ambiguous hope, never clearly involving the assurance of personal survival. Hence Greek philosophy, having promised rational certainty about the supernatural, failed to deliver where it touched man at the deepest level; deep longings remained unsatisfied and forceful questions were unsolved.

Rome borrowed from the Greeks not only speculative metaphysics, but the motives for literature and art. Stoic-

---

4. Edwyn R. Bevan noted three voids in the Greek view which the Hebraic view of the world would confront in a striking manner (see note 10, below). They are seen in the facts that "(1) God, when once the primitive and naive polytheism had been left behind, tended to become immovable Being, to which men might indeed strive to attain, but which did not do particular acts in the world-process; (2) the world-process was a vain eternal recurrence, a circular movement, leading nowhere; and (3) deliverance was attained by the individual when he detached himself in soul from the world, not through his incorporation in a Divine community of the blessed" (in *The Legacy of Israel*. Bevan and Singer, eds., 50. Oxford: Clarendon Press, 1928, 1948 reprinting).

5. S. Angus pointedly contrasts the Hebrew Old Testament view with that of the classic Greek philosophy of time. Judaism was professedly an exclusive revealed religion whose "unequivocal message of a divine purpose working itself out in the events of time and advancing surely towards a goal supplied an inspiring world-view to those who were dissatisfied with the Hellenic, especially Stoic, view of the world-process as a never-ending recurrent series of cycles which merely repeated the past without any very definite aim or consummation. . . (and) a wholesome corrective to the world view of those who under later Platonic influence removed the world of reality into the supernal realm and belittled the mightiest events of history as symbols of the eternal world. . . Thus the Jews gave to these centuries in the throes of change and revival a concrete present value to the very history of which they were a notable part" (*The Religious Quests of the Graeco-Roman World*, 55-56. London: John Murray, 1929).

ism, the deterministic pantheism of ancient times, provided a doctrine of man universally linked to the one divine spirit — a world empire of such beings. The Stoic emphasis held special appeal on its practical as much as on its speculative side; the breakdown of the Greek rationale fixed interest on ethics rather than on metaphysics. But Neo-Platonism proved most representative of later pagan philosophy, and as a speculative view it was in some ways the product of cravings which the earlier Greek philosophy had left unsatisfied. In place of the rational approach to God which the classic philosophy had carried out with a misplaced confidence in man, Neo-Platonism substituted a rational approach which culminated in an ecstatic, mystic experience. Not only was rational contemplation superseded, but the way to God became mediatorial, the divine ideas being regarded as gods which are emanations from the One and which stand between the One and the human soul. Hence Platonic-Aristotelian obscurity, precisely in the area at which it demanded clarity — concerning, that is the nature of the supernatural — issued in later philosophies in a concentration on the ethical more than on the metaphysical, in a movement away from the significance of reason for philosophy and religion, and in a view which made room for multiplied intermediaries. When Platonism made its reappearance, in Neo-Platonism, it failed to win an upper hand against Stoic pantheism. While no naturalistic culture was attempted in ancient times, and the classic philosophy seemed to have made its case for the impossibility of succeeding in such a venture, yet the universe synthesis of the Greek idealists was powerless to forestall the cultural deterioration.

Stoicism and Neo-Platonism were not, indeed, the only options. "Platonism, Stoicism, Neo-Platonism, Mithraism,

Manicheism, and Gnosticism, these names, taken for simplicity's sake," remarked Henry Osborn Taylor, "serve to indicate the mind and temper of the educated world in which Christianity was spreading."[6] The classic synthesis had fallen apart, and the ideal of synthesis appeared to have been lost for a time in the drift toward differentiation.

Yet in the third and fourth centuries "the common yearning of the Graeco-Roman world," as Taylor put it, "was for an approach to God."[7] Into the void, which the Greek confidence both in natural reason and in mysticism had failed to overcome, Christianity moved with power, first on a purely personal level with the preaching of the apostolic Gospel, and then more and more as a social force also.

---

6. Henry Osborn Taylor, *The Mediaeval Mind*, I, 50. (Cambridge: Harvard University Press, 1949, 4th ed., 5th printing).

7. *Ibid.*, I. 54. Regarding the providential preparation of the world of antiquity for the Christian message, the reader may recall Edmond Pressensé's words: "Although the Gospel is not, as has been affirmed, the product of anterior civilizations — a mere compound of Greek and Oriental elements — it is not the less certain that it brings to the human mind the satisfaction vainly sought by it in the East as in the West. . . The night of paganism had its stars to light it, but. . .they called to the Morning-star which stood over Bethlehem. If we regard philosophy as a preparation for Christianity, instead of seeking in it a substitute for the Gospel, we shall not need to overstate its grandeur in order to estimate its real value" (*Religions Before Christ.*) David R. Breed's volume on *A History of the Preparation of the World for Christ*, (New York: Fleming H. Revell Company, 1893) is valuable as a comprehensive survey in this realm of thought. Some useful suggestions are also to be found in B. F. Cocker's chapter on "The Propaedeutic Office of Greek Philosophy" in his volume on *Christianity and Greek Philosophy* (New York: Harper & Brothers, 1870). Cocker assesses the pagan spirit too positively, but he is properly aware of the reality of general revelation when he affirms: "To despise the religions of the ancient world, to sneer at the efforts and achievements of the old philosophers, or even to cut them off in thought from all relation to the plans and movements of that Providence which has cared for, and watched over, and pitied, and guided all the nations of the earth, is to refuse to comprehend Christianity itself" (*ibid.*, vii).

2. The Medieval Mind

Western thought need not have been divided into more than two periods, into the ancient and modern eras, were it not for the great fact of the coming of Jesus Christ into the world. The appearance of the founder of Christianity results, finally, in the tripartite division of western thought. The series of events central to the Christian faith, which issued in calendrical dating from the time of Christ, cannot be grasped realistically, unless one senses the decided contrast involved therein with both the ancient and modern world views. The world frame before His coming, and the recent modern mind which has stood in revolt against cardinal outlines of the medieval outlook, cannot be assimilated to the Biblical outlook. It is necessary to partition western thought in three directions because the genius of the medieval outlook refuses any self-reduction to the ancient or modern minds.

The medieval world and life view was not in all respects, however, entirely new. A religion claiming absolute revelation, and hence an authority universal in time and space, must explain the past, no less than the present and future.[8] Christianity came into the world as the fulfillment of all genuine religious desire, but especially as the completion of

8. The absence of any conviction of assured revelation in Greek philosophy, which tended to identify revelation with contemplative intuition; was of the utmost importance for the ancient world. "Greek philosophy," wrote Angus, "did not feel compelled, like Hebrew prophetism and the Christian mission, to 'evangelize' mankind at large" (*ibid*, 102-103). Contemporary humanism, which seeks to promote social concern for mankind apart from the Christian message of God's electing love, could learn a much-needed lesson from history at this point.

the Hebrew claim to special revelation.[9] It was not without
the closest affinity, therefore, to the Old Testament view of
God and world, with its distinctive explanation of the movement of things.[10] That the one eternal and sovereign God
created the world and all things by divine fiat; that man
was created in the divine image, and hence possessed a distinctive dignity, being made for personal fellowship with
the Deity; that man, by voluntary revolt, fell from original
righteousness into a state of moral and spiritual revolt; that

---

9. Cocker emphasized that "Christianity did not break suddenly upon
the world as a new commencement altogether unconnected with the past,
and wanting in all points of sympathy and contact with the then present.
It proceeded along lines of thought which had been laid through ages
of preparation... It was, in fact, the consummation of the whole moral
and religious history of the world" (*Ibid.*, 462). Cocker had in view
the more general preparation of history for the advent of Christ. But
the incarnation was not the fulfillment of world religion in the same
sense that it was the fulfillment of Hebrew theology, not even in a
lesser degree. For the work of preparation among the Jews was u-
nique, being predicated upon a special revelation, and upon the divine relation to a people singly chosen to be a means for the communication of
true religion to men who had fallen away from their spiritual heritage.
If Hebrew-Christian thought has sometimes gone to extremes, by a
denial of any supervision of providence outside the Biblical movement,
the modern tendency, that of the absorption of the divine movement
among the Hebrews to the general movement of religion, is the far
worse error, although both extremities need to be guarded against.

10. Edwyn R. Bevan singles out as the three respects in which the
Hebrew view offered a contrast to the Greek view, the following: "(1)
an apprehension of God as righteous Will, Some One who does definite
'mighty acts' in the world-process; and hence (2) a conception of the
world-process as process in Time, which embodies a Divine plan beginning in God's mighty acts of creation and leading up to a great consummation in the future; (3) an association of the Divine plan with a Divine community, a 'people of God' chosen to be the vehicle of God's
purpose, so that the ultimate consummation is a communal bliss, the
community redeemed, blessed, and glorious" (*The Legacy of Israel*,
50).

salvation is impossible of attainment by human effort but is a provision of the God of holy love, who through His prophets promised a vicarious mediation from the divine side; that the provision of salvation is to be realized within history itself by the God who in a special way reveals Himself to His chosen people — what are these, but affirmations which stand at the core of the Old Testament, no less than of Biblical Christianity?

But the Hebrew revelation looks ahead to the future, as divine promise hushed in expectation of its fulfillment. The Old Testament necessarily awaits its own supersession; it bears latent within, the pledge of its future development and consummation. Christianity, if not wholly new, was not shrinkable to the Hebraic revelation; such a view would cancel out entirely the phenomenon of the entrance of Jesus Christ into history. From the New Testament perspective Judaism lacks its climax, and halts short of its proper terminus and crown.

Stressing this irreducibility of Christianity, Angus wrote of its appearance "as a new religion, new not in point of time only, but in character and power, 'the spirit of life in Christ Jesus,' and with a startling claim to possess truth not through an idea or a theory of knowledge, but in a person. . . Christianity was a view of the world. . .and a way of Life with the inestimable advantage over all its competitors of possessing an historical and personal centre in the person of Jesus. . .(who) proved potent to awaken moral enthusiasms and release the perennial means of renewal through the course of Christian history. Jesus could never be presented as an abstraction or reduced to a beautiful myth."[11] The central personality of the Hebrew-Christian revelation confronted all humanity, not alone by offering a pure theoretical revelation about God and man, but by proclaiming Himself the deliverer who answers to man's need of reconciliation, and standing as mediator, by His vicarious sacrifice, between the divine and the human. "No pagan philosophy, not Platonism or any system that came after it," wrote Henry Osborn Taylor, "had afforded an incentive for concentration of desire equal to that presented in the person and the precepts of Jesus."[12] The saving word of God is centered in His Person, and any tampering with the outlines of that Figure could not but imperil the whole structure of Christianity.

While, therefore, the Hebrew-Christian view ranged itself formally on the side of the Greek idealistic case against naturalism, it stood opposed at the same time to the classic emphasis on the rational competence, in the realm of metaphysics, of the natural man in his state of sin; to the dualistic reduction of evil from a moral to a metaphysical problem; to the failure to identify the moral realm with the will of God; to the emptying of history of redemptive significance.

---

11. Angus, *ibid.*, 93, 94. The passage does not sufficiently emphasize, however, Christianity's continuity with the Old Testament. Instead of appearing as a new religion, Christianity appeared as Old Testament religion, developed in terms of increased revelation. But the increase was staggering. "Tame and empty all the holy legends. . .must have seemed to any man reading or listening to the still recent story of Jesus' sufferings — the last journey to Jerusalem, the last anxious supper, the hours of despair in Gethsemane, and the death on the cross," wrote Oswald Spengler. "Christianity is the one religion in the history of the world in which the fate of a man of the immediate present has become the emblem and the central point of the whole Creation" (*The Decline of the West,* II, 212. New York: Alfred A. Knopf, 1945).

12. Henry Osborn Taylor, *ibid.*, 58.

Christianity opposed itself to naturalism, that is, by a revelational view of men and things which also countered idealism.[13]   The essential differences between the classic Greek
and the medieval frameworks will become immediately apparent if, pausing for a moment, one anticipates the impression upon Plato and Aristotle, could they but have
overheard a medieval catechist reciting the so-called Apostles
Creed.   The emphasis upon the absolute sovereignty of God
and His creation of all things out of nothing, upon the exclusive mediation of Jesus Christ, upon the entrance of the
divine into history, upon the crucifixion and resurrection of
Christ as a central article of faith, upon the forgiveness of
sins, let alone other elements of the *Credo,* would have stag-
gered the imagination of the Greek idealists.   The essence

13. It was all too easy for subsequent thought, in view of the anthropocentric lodging of Greek philosophy, to dismiss its transcendental
elements in the name of sheer postulation.   Ernst Curtius' moving
paragraph on how "the greatest service. . .which any Hellene could
perform for his country was to combat, by means of a deeper and more
serious process of thought, that of the Sophists, which endangered the
best possessions of the people, and to drive from the field this one-sided
cultivation of the reason, which was altogether undesirous of attaining,
by means of a studious research which laid bare the final causes of moral
life, to any absolutely valid truth" (*The History of Greece,* IV, 139-140.
New York: Charles Scribner's Sons, 1899, tr. by A. W. Ward) has this
very sort of denouement in the assertion that "against the false subjectivity of the Sophists there existed no other resource than that
higher subjectivity which Socrates asserted — the subjectivity based
upon serious self-examination, whereby alone could be obtained a valid
standard for the gifts of the mind" (*ibid.,* 164).   So R. W. Livingstone,
after conceding the moral contribution of Greek thought, and the importance especially of the doctrine of the Mean and the Stoic ideal of
virtue, denied that these are by any means an essential of the Greek
genius (*The Greek Genius and Its Mean to Us,* 25-27. London: Oxford University Press, 1924, 2nd ed.).   The coldness of Greek philosophical morality, in contrast with revelational theism and ethics, with its
emphasis on the self-disclosing God, is the key to this absence of perpetual vitality in the ancient outlook.

of the Christian view involved, therefore, elements which distinguished the Biblical outlook as unique, much as it was ranged formally on the side of the classic view in its opposition to naturalism.[14]

The Hebrew-Christian outlook consequently merits its own statement of cardinal tenets. It affirms, as James Orr well summarized,[15] the existence of a personal, ethical, self-revealing God; the creation of the world by God, His immanent presence in it, and His holy and wise government of it for moral ends; the spiritual nature and dignity of man — his creation in the Divine image, and destination to bear the likeness of God in a perfected relation of sonship; the fact of the sin and disorder of the world, not as something belonging to the Divine idea of it, and inhering in it by necessity, but as something which has entered it by the voluntary turning aside of man from his allegiance to his Creator, and from the path of his normal development; the historical self-revelation of God to the patriarchs and in the line of Israel, and, as brought to light by this, a gracious purpose of God for the salvation of the world, centering in

---

14. This is not fully appreciated by writers who, like Angus, take the view that "Christianity proved unable to discover a method of coming to terms with or appropriating ancient culture without rending the rich fabric of Graeco-Roman civilization" (*ibid.*, x). For it was not due to a reckless repudiation of Graeco-Roman culture, a needless uprooting of wheat and tares alike, but rather to the inner genius of Christianity working itself out in conscious judgment on the ancient view, that the upheaval must be traced.

15. James Orr, *The Christian View of God and the World,* 32-34 (New York: Charles Scribner's Sons, 1897). Orr spoke of these propositions as the "minimal postulates" of the Biblical view, but he did not intend by the word "postulates" what that word, since Kant's day, is commonly taken to mean — i. e., the spiritual demand of universal human nature; rather, for Orr, these propositional truths were rooted in special divine revelation.

Jesus Christ,[16] His son, and the new Head of humanity; that Jesus Christ was not mere man, but the eternal Son of God — a truly Divine Person — who in the fulness of time took upon Him our humanity, and who, on the ground that in Him as man there dwells the fulness of the Godhead bodily, is to be honoured, worshipped, and trusted, even as God is; the redemption of the world through the great act of atonement, to be appropriated by faith, and availing for all who do not wilfully withstand and reject its grace; that the historical aim of Christ's work was the founding of a Kingdom of God on earth, which includes not only the spiritual salvation of individuals, but a new order of society; that history has a goal, and that the present order of things will be terminated by the appearance of the Son of Man for judgment, the resurrection of the dead, and the final separation of righteous and wicked. Whether one turns to the synoptic evangelists or to the writers of the

16. The dating of time from the birth of Christ, introduced in Italy in the 6th century by the Roman abbot Dionysius the Little, has frequently provoked the complaint that such dating from an intermediate period of history involves the inconvenience of the double manner of reckoning forward and backward. But that is precisely what the Biblical view of history required — a Janus-faced chronology of salvation history, which moved from promise to fulfillment and identified the coming of Jesus Christ as the fulness of time. Karl Löwith has noted: "Pre-Christian as well as post-Christian paganism reckons historical time from a *beginning*...usually...a decisive political event...The Jews, too, reckon historical time from a beginning — the world's creation — though in views of an *eschaton*. What is particular to the Christian time-reckoning is that it counts from a *central* event, which occurred when the time had been fulfilled. For the Jews, the central event is still in the future, and the expectation of the Messiah divides for them all the time into a present and a future aeon. For the Christian the dividing line in the history of salvation is no longer a mere *futurum* but a *perfectum prae-sens*, the accomplished advent of Jesus Christ. With regard to this central event the time is reckoned *forward as well as backward*. The years of the history B. C. continuously decrease while the years A. D. increase toward an end-time" (*Meaning in History*, 182 (Chicago: The University of Chicago Press, 1949).

epistles, whether it is to the early church fathers or to later exponents of Christianity like Augustine, or Anselm, or Aquinas, or Luther and Calvin, or to the modern movements which mirror historic Christianity, this formulation will serve as an admirable summary of the distinctive outlines of the medieval view.

The reduction of Christianity to something less than its inner claim was a phenomenon with which it has had to contend, not merely in modern times,[17] but throughout the medieval period as well, as the movement known in church history as the Reformation makes plain. It can hardly be maintained that the Middle Ages issued in the fullest sense in a Christian culture, for the problem of assimilating a collapsed civilization is not easily met. Christianity did not become a universal dynamic possession; sometimes its inner message was lost in a well of emotion, or again a semi-pagan approach was retained, for all the uplift of the new faith, and elements derived from a pagan environment were only outwardly transformed by Christian necessities. Even if paganism was a dissipated and lost cause, so that by the fourth century the best minds in both East and West were ranged on the side of Christianity, the energy and vitality

---

17. For a century, religious modernism has sought to find a different "essence of Christianity" than that suggested here, but in the end this effort, however great the names identified with it, ended in failure. Walter Marshall Horton had to concede, in 1933, when he acknowledged the breakdown of liberalism as a system of theology, that J. Gresham Machen had made his case, in *Christianity and Liberalism,* that the historical records of the Christian movement were not on the side of the liberal reinterpretation (*Realistic Theology,* 3. New York: Harper and Brothers, 1934). Liberalism has never felt the force of the fact that the early antagonists of supernatural Christianity did not employ the modern objections. It never occurred to Celsus that the New Testament is a gradual reconstruction of a primitive tradition in which the so-called "liberal Christ" was transformed; his criticism proceeded, rather, on ground which was frankly philosophical.

of Biblical faith was weakened often by the mere recasting
of pagan motifs, rather than their replacement in terms of
a thorough Christianity.   The crass superstition and religious intolerance to which Roman Catholicism accommodated
itself, moreover, and the needless years of darkness in the
wake of the passing of the Graeco-Roman culture,[18] the
ecclesiastical institutionalizing of Christianity, the emphasis
on credal subscription apart from genuine spiritual decision,
the ascetic and monastic movements, the supplanting of the
exclusive mediation of Christ — these unhappy perversions
are an indubitable element of medieval times, which modern
naturalism expounds with eloquence, howbeit out of genuine
philosophical perspective.   The Christian ideal may not have
been fully realized, but Biblical Christanity itself held out
little encouragement for a total realization within history,
prior to the eschatological future, of the kingdom of God;
the Roman Catholic identification of the divine kingdom
with the church only tended to obscure the radical Biblical
doctrine of sin and redemption.

Nonetheless, there emerged in medieval times a distinctive culture, a synthesis in which the tensions of time and
eternity were pointed for their resolution to the Biblical
view of life.   The segregation of medieval history, of medieval philosophy, of a medieval in contrast with the ancient
and modern minds, is not a wholly artificial thing.   No less

------

18. It is only the yardstick of phantasy, however, which measures
the "dark ages" as a thousand year period, for recent gains in historical
knowledge make plain that the exaggerated estimates of earlier decades
need to be shortened considerably.   But no alert student of medieval
history can relate that era without some real sympathy for the revolt
from the church of the Middle Ages, so far as it was motivated by
repugnance for a formalistic and sacramental religion, for the alien
papal monarch of Rome, and for the encouragement which Roman
Catholicism offered to superstition and magic.

than in our times, a certain way of discerning facts and of appraising their value and significance distinguished the medieval era, so that diversity of outlook and inner conflict was a phenomenon secondary to the basic intellectual temperament. The medieval genius worked itself out in a constructive spirit which, in contrast with the modern cultural disunity, creates constantly in subsequent centuries a longing for its reincarnation, even if in a purified form freed of the perversions of Roman ecclesiasticism. That synthesis was, in intent, theological rather than philosophical; it centered in the conviction that the self-revealing God had rescued mankind from both hell and pagan savagery. "The medieval spirit was dominated throughout," as expressed by one scholar, whose sympathies were not with the past, "by the conception of a supreme harmony subordinating the natural to the supernatural order, a harmony in which all the activities of the soul, religion, philosophy, art, science, and conduct were united in the realization of the ideal of the City of God. The Christian thus had, in the last analysis, little need for a philosophy — the questions which really interested him and the problems which were of supreme importance to his destiny were all answered, and his needs all satisfied, by his theology and its concrete manifestation in his personal religious life."[19] Nothing can be clearer than that the medieval mind related to Christ, at least in intention, not only theology and worship, but philosophy, government, art, music and literature. It did so not in the name of speculation, but in the name of revelation; not in terms of human initiative, but of divine disclosure; not in the spirit of groping for God's forgiveness, but rather of expressing its grati-

19. C. R. S. Harris in C. S. Crump and E. F. Jacob's (eds.) *The Legacy of the Middle Ages,* 252 (Oxford: Clarendon Press, 1926, reprinted 1943).

tude for the divinely provided gift of salvation, and of an awaiting of the complete vindication of God's promises. "The desire of the Kingdom of Heaven was," as Taylor expressed it, "a master-motive such as no previous idealism had offered. It would bring into conformity with itself not only all the practical considerations of life, but verily the whole human desire to know. . . Its decree was this: The knowledge which men need and should desire is that which will help them to save and perfect their soul for the Kingdom of God."[20]

Historians do not properly write of the collapse of medieval culture — even though Oswald Spengler does so — for it is related to the modern rather by way of gradual transition. In that transition a change more radical was involved than in the ancient replacement of philosophical idealism by Biblical theism, since both these views affirmed the reality of the supernatural. But the modern transition ends with the denial of the supernatural, whether it is affirmed on speculative or on revelational ground. And to this exchange, the scholastic philosophy of the Middle Ages itself unwittingly contributed. Medieval philosophy is not without warning voices that scholastic philosophy, and especially the great Thomistic synthesis of the thirteenth century, had stated

20. Taylor, *ibid.*, I, 58f. "Salvation was the master Christian motive," added Taylor, "The Gospel of Christ was a gospel of salvation unto eternal life. . .the self-sacrifice of divine love, not without warnings touching its reception". . . "The intellectual interests of the Christian Fathers are not to be classified under categories of desire to know, for the sake of knowledge, but under categories of desire to be saved, and to that end possess knowledge in its saving forms.". . "Philosophy itself — the general inquiry for final knowledge — no longer had an independent existence." . . "Patristic philosophy consisted in the formulation of Christian doctrine, which in theory was an elucidating of the truth of Scripture" (*ibid.*, 61, 62, 68, 70).

the Biblical view in a self-defeating way. The Thomistic synthesis of science, philosophy and theology involved such an obscuring of the inner genius of Christianity that sooner or later the revelational view must lose its hold — not by any inner necessity of Biblical theism, but simply because the inner spirit of that view had not been properly grasped by the scholastics. The Protestant Reformation was, on its theological side, in part, a protest against the manner in which medieval Catholicism had formulated the Christian answer to the problem of religious knowledge. While the great reformers, Luther and Calvin, did not by any means confine their criticisms of Romanism to religious epistemology, they were unsparing in their contention — shared at points before them by scholastics like Duns Scotus — that Christianity was presented to the modern world in most unsatisfactory and self-defeating terms by the Thomistic relating of reason and faith.[21]

3. The Modern Mind

The modern mind is no bosom companion of the dominant ideologies which preceded it; of that there can be little doubt. The post-Renaissance, post-scientific philosophy of the western world has distinctive differences which forbid its identification with the classic views of either ancient or medieval times. The phrases "modern culture," the "scientific era," and their like, are not empty catchwords; they stand for an inner spirit which has forced Christianity to

21. For a sympathetic treatment of the Thomistic synthesis, see Etienne Gilson's *Reason and Revelation in the Middle Ages;* for a critical treatment, from a neo-supernaturalistic rather than Protestant orthodox view, see Emil Brunner's *Revelation and Reason;* for some comments by the writer, see *Remaking the Modern Mind*, 200ff., 230ff., and *The Protestant Dilemma,* 43-58.

fight for its very life.[22] Ancient classic thought would have been drawn similarly into battle for survival had that still been the prevailing philosophy; for the modern mind, in its outworking, becomes an alternative to both the Greek idealistic and the Hebrew-Christian theistic views. The central calendrical reference was now to become not the Christian divide, but, in the spirit of Copernicus and Darwin, the vast antiquity in the hidden recesses of the evolutionary process.

It is no less difficult, however, to date the rise of the modern mind than that of the ancient and medieval. Just as Greek idealism must acknowledge that the conviction of the priority of mind over matter did not begin with the Platonists or Aristotelians, but is somehow implied, however dimly, in all primitive religious belief, and just as the exposition of the Christian view requires the Hebrew revelation for its setting, so modern thought is not without any antecedents whatever. For the first time, however, particular emphases which appeared here and there among ancient

---

22. A selection of book titles during the past generation includes such revealing subjects as: P. T. Forsyth's *Positive Preaching and the Modern Mind* (1907), G. A. Johnston Ross, *et al.*, *Religion and the Modern Mind* (1908), Shailer Mathews' *The Gospel and the Modern Man* (1910), William Temple's *The Faith and Modern Thought* (1910), Ezra A. Cook's *Christian Faith for Men of Today* (1913), Rudolph Eucken's *Can We Still Be Christians?* (1914), Charles R. Brown, *et. al.*, *Christianity and Modern Thought* (1924), W. R. Matthews' *The Gospel and the Modern Mind* (1925), Charles Gore's *Can We Then Believe?* (1926), Ernest DeWitt Burton's *Christianity in The Modern World* (1927), Charles C. Cooper (ed.), *Religion and the Modern Mind* (1929), R. J. Campbell's *Christian Faith in Modern Light* (1932), George Arthur Buttrick's *The Christian Fact and Modern Doubt* (1934), and William E. Hocking, *et. al.*, *The Church and the New World Mind* (1944). Nobody can scan this list of titles without feeling that the modern mind somehow placed Christianity along with religion generally on the defensive in such a way as to force a fight for survival.

thinkers became, in the modern era, the basis upon which the rearing of a culture was attempted. By this provision of an alien frame of reference for the interpretation of nature and of the meaning of life and thought, modern culture furnishes in its naturalistic basis a stark and irreducible contrast to the outlooks of ancient and medieval times.

From the modern side frequently comes the emphasis that the only essential division of western thought is into its pre-scientific and post-scientific eras. The distinctively modern features are held to be opposed about equally to the ancient and medieval outlooks. Those older frameworks may have seemed opposed to past generations, whereas representative modern thinkers regard them simply as variants of a single alternative against which later thought rebels — so radically different is this modern conception of things, which strikes alike at the frames of reference on which ancient and medieval cultures were predicated.

This may indeed appear an oversimplification. Has not the modern era, it may be asked with good reason, had its great theistic and idealistic traditions in philosophy, which have contended vigourously against any naturalistic reductionism? And assuredly the story of modern philosophy cannot be written without prominent attention to the supernaturalistic schools of thought, from Descartes to Hocking, Flewelling and Brightman. But that does not require a revision of what has been said. Had modern culture been erected, in its final expression, on an idealistic view, then the pattern of western thought would have consisted not of three contrastive periods, but of cultural expressions of philosophical idealism bisected by the medieval expression of Biblical supernaturalism. But it has not been so. For it is the naturalistic philosophy which has worked itself out to dominance and victory on the modern scene. Post-Christian idealism found itself unable to score the victory over naturalism which both ancient idealism for a time, and Christianity for a millennium and a half, had been able to effect. For reasons to be related, emphases which had been anticipated by ancient naturalism, but which classic Greek thought drove for several centuries into the background, and which Christianity banished into the shadows for more than fifteen hundred years, came now to prevail over the modern philosophic scene, and to assert themselves as the influential categories of recent western culture.

The modern mind reached its naturalistic terminus not at once but by a gradual process, because it needed first to emancipate itself from concepts which once were thought to belong properly to its perspective, but which more and more were seen to have been borrowed, by an overlooked debt, from the Hebrew-Christian view of things. That is why Renaissance thought had first its spiritual and then its secular expressions. Just as in medieval times, Christian culture in its partial realization did not become an actuality for many centuries and yet its beginnings were rooted in the singular events of B. C. 6 - 30 A. D., so too the rise of modern philosophy with Descartes in 1600, and the Renaissance preparations for it, are the seeds which, when finally the plants revert to type, are seen to have sown the naturalistic outgrowths which in our day men fear to be the harvest which matures just before the season of nihilism sets in.

THE
PARTITIONS OF WESTERN THOUGHT:
MODERN

II

The Partitions of Western Thought: Modern

THE central postulate of the modern mind, in its final expression, has been the ultimacy of nature.

This central affirmation carries with it much else that is important. To declare that nature alone is the ultimate real, so that all reality takes its rise in and through differentiations of the natural world, is to declare at the same time that man is essentially an animal and that moral distinctions are only subjective and relative. It is to deny, that is, the reality of anything — gods, souls, values, or anything else — unsubject to time and change.

By this central postulate, the modern mind places itself definitely over against the ancient and medieval minds. From the standpoint of both earlier views, when taken together, the distinctive modern prejudice is its denial of the reality of the supernatural. From the standpoint of the Biblical view alone — deliberately we do not say, of the medieval view, since scholastic philosophy was also guilty, though in a lesser degree, of obscuring this feature[1] — the distinctive modern trait is its denial of special divine revelation.

That modern philosophy, in its beginnings. was anything but overtly naturalistic is, as we have already stated, beside

---

1. Since the Thomistic synthesis erected the first story of its case for theism in terms of Aristotelian cosmology, it arrived philosophically at the existence of God in such a way as to conceal entirely up to this point the principle of special revelation. This will be expanded in the following chapter.

the point. What concerns us especially is the pattern of thought around which the attempt has been made to rear a homogeneous culture. In modern times, it is the naturalistic emphasis which has come to victory in the propaganda centers of the West and, finally, in the Orient also. Karl Marx sat, as is well known, under Hegel, not under an Indian Swami. In its final mood, the modern mind, sometimes implicitly, sometimes explicitly, declared against the reality of the supernatural. That the world of nature is the prime reality, that the solution of all crucial problems will come by making the space-time universe, inclusive of man, the legitimate center of speculative interest, that it is the natural order above all with which a modern man must be familiar — what are these but characteristically modern notions, which came by the nineteenth and twentieth centuries to serve as the unexpressed ultimates presupposed in the educative centers of western culture, in western Europe and the British Isles and the United States before those, in turn, of Soviet Russia?

The distinctive modern reference therefore is not empirical science. By and of itself, the modern interest in science would require no division of mind from the ancient and medieval eras. The prestige of science may be combined equally well with an idealistic or a Biblical theistic view, and any claim that the modern mind arises as a necessary distinction because of our era of scientific research is clearly debatable. Naturalism has illegitimately assumed that modern science implies the naturalistic philosophy of science. Science and the supernatural are not intrinsic opposites; in ancient and medieval times alike gifted men have insisted on the reality and irreducibility of the natural and the supernatural. In the Greek era idealism no less than natural ism manifested an interest in science.[2] The relationship of Christianity to modern science, whatever may be said of the errors of the medieval church, is by no means wholly negative. The early scientists of the modern era were men of devout Christian conviction, for one thing.[3] Even more important, it may be questioned seriously whether the scientific enterprise as we know it would have arisen, had it not been for the Hebrew-Christian framework which stood behind the modern interest in nature. The ancient polytheistic world views, obviously enough, afforded no encouragement for seeking a unitary power or principle in explanation of all phenomena. The classic Greek thinkers, in their appeal to an unchanging supernatural rationale in explanation of the changing world of nature, were more compatible with the scientific impetus, but here too there were retarding elements. Their interpretation of matter, for example, was radically different from the Christian view of a creation in complete control of an infinite Mind; matter for Plato could

2. Although the materialist Democritus anticipated the modern chemical analysis of quantitative elements, both the Pythagoreans and Plato had stressed the mathematical structure of nature, later revived in the Copernican emphasis on a universe conceived in terms of geometrical units. Of Aristotle, the editor of a volume of selections from his writings wrote that "he was an Ionian, a member of that branch of the Greek race which was responsible for the origin of the philosophy of nature in the school of Miletus, and which was distinguished from other branches by a devouring curiosity about the facts of nature, and their explanation. . . He was from first to last. . .an observer of the facts of nature, a man for whom no problem was too detailed to whet his curiosity" (W. D. Ross (ed.), *Aristotle: Selections,* v. New York: Charles Scribner's Sons, 1927).

3. It is quite the fashion among naturalists to trace the beginning of nineteenth century mechanistic science to Newton, and then to argue that he combined his scientific views uncritically with the traditional theology. But the fact is rather the reverse; Newton was not a marginal Christian, but combined his faith with a scientific interest which was sometimes formulated uncritically in relationship to it, so that what to Newton was an abstractionist view of reality came rather easily to be viewed by some of his successors as a complete explanation.

resist the changeless divine ideas, whereas for Aristotle it possessed an over-potency for form. In both cases, the eternality of matter gave it a relative independence over against an all-embracing rationale. Moreover, Plato's philosophy obscured the possibility of explanation in terms of one ultimate reference, since he did not unambiguously identify the realm of eternal ideas with Deity and, beyond that, invoked also at times the activity of the Demiurge. But the uncompromising monotheism of the Hebrew-Christian tradition, coupled with the insistence upon a divine creation of the universe, so that the entire structure of finite being finds its rationale in an orderly, benevolent, and sovereign divine Mind, furnished the background for the modern confidence that science, wherever it penetrated, would find the universe to be meaningful. Christianity, therefore, is more the mother than the avowed enemy of modern science. Whatever unpleasant chapters may be contained in church history, recording the ill-advised opposition of religious leaders to scientific insights and advances,[4] these must not be allowed to conceal what is the actual fact, that the deepest concern on the part of churchmen has always been not science, but that illegitimate proclamation in the name of science of anti-supernaturalism — a fear which subsequent history has proved only to be abundantly justified.[5] Bettex's closing words, in his volume on this theme of theologico-scientific

---

4. These accounts frequently are lifted out of all historical perspective by modern antisupernaturalists. The Copernican controversy did not turn on an appeal to sensation as against revelation; not against revelation, for the Scriptures nowhere condition the Hebrew-Christian view on the astronomic centrality of the earth; not to sensation, for humanists like Edwin A. Burtt have made the point that "contemporary empiricists, had they lived in the sixteenth century, would have been the first to scoff out of court the new philosophy of the universe" (*The Metaphysical Foundations of Modern Physical Science*, 25. London: Routledge and Kegan Paul, Ltd, 1949, Rev. ed.)

conflict, were aptly chosen: "The Christian does not believe
in opposition to science and in spite of science; but he be-
lieves, in consequence of . . .knowledge, that the science of
faith better explains the past and present order of things,
and is, for that reason, truer and more scientific than the
science of unbelief."[6]

Even in a more striking manner, than in supplying the
atmosphere which made the rise of modern science possible,
did the Hebrew-Christian view stand in the background of
the modern mind. For it did not at once remove to a marginal role all concern with theological and moral ultimates;
it did not at once concentrate attention on the natural rather
than the supernatural realm in unraveling the persistent
problems of thought and life. Only by a gradual inner
compulsion of its own dialectic did it find its way, from
Cartesian dualism, to positivistic monism. Modern philosophy began, in Descartes, with a species of theism that was
already far removed from Biblical Christianity, but it began
also with a type of philosophy that was likewise far removed
from the positivism of Comte and Dewey. The reason for
its beginning at an intermediary point is that it did not at
once perceive that, in its rupture with Biblical Christianity,
in which it carried further a process of separation already

5. This bias against religion, in the name of "unbiased science," is
illustrated by Andrew D. White's two-volume work on *A History of
the Warfare of Science With Theology in Christendom* (New York:
D. Appleton and Company, 1913). On the one hand, theology becomes
a comprehensive term which includes every type of dogmatic and even
arbitrary exegesis of Scripture, no less than the whole realm of mythology, and hence is represented constantly in its worst light; on the
other, science is persistently portrayed without the slightest suggestion
that Christianity has had for its enemy not science in any of its assured results but rather that speculative dogmatism and arbitrary interpretation of science which equates an alien philosophy of science with
science itself.

6. F. Bettex, *Science and Christianity*, 326 (Cincinnati: Jennings
& Pye, 1901).

implicit in medieval Scholasticism,[7] it still retained vital elements absorbed unconsciously from Biblical theism, and not at all integral to the avenue of understanding which modern thought had charted for itself in its speculative approach to reality.

But if Biblical Christianity stood thus in the background of the rise and beginnings of modern philosophy, the course of speculative thought itself would take the route more and more of a conscious revolt against these Biblical elements. If there is one ingredient in modern philosophy which made quite inevitable its removal from supernaturalistic to naturalistic terrain, it is the fact of its rejection of the principle of special divine revelation, i. e., of the Biblical miraculous. The early theistic and idealistic traditions, admittedly, sought to conserve what they considered the essential features of the Biblical view of God and man, of history and nature, despite the sacrifice of the principle of once-for-all Biblical revelation. They bore the stamp, that is to say, of their post-Christian, rather than pre-Christian appearance. But they bore this stamp not alone in the aspects of Biblical Christianity which they saluted; equally much, they witnessed to their post-medieval orientation by the features which they rejected

7. Evangelical Protestantism since the Reformation, in its discerning philosophical statements, has emphasized the judgment with which the "eternal Mind" stands upon ancient and modern history, and upon medieval history as well. There is no glib tendency on the part of Reformation Protestantism to minimize the modern indictment of the medieval church's encouragement of superstition and its corruption of a pure Christianity, tendencies which continue still despite a margin of improvement issuing from the Roman Counter-Reformation. From the standpoint of Biblical theology, the issues are no longer multiple: Greek idealism, medieval supernaturalism, modern naturalism; the modern man cannot stay with the latter without evaporating the essence of human existence and activity, nor can he return to the others because philosophical idealism is profoundly discontinuous with God's self-revelation and because Roman Catholicism is too leavened with speculative elements which conceal the vitality of special revelation.

— always, of course, as "secondary" and "marginal" phases, and never as elementals. More and more, in the unfolding of modern thought, it became apparent that the rejection of the Biblical miraculous involved the rejection of much more than modern thought had suspected, that it implicated indeed the whole view of God, of man, of history, of nature. In fact, the rejection of special revelation, when once it is articulated from the modern perspective, was seen to proceed from assumptions which made it difficult any longer to cling to the reality of the supernatural. The transition to modern idealism was made in a spirit which involved the setting aside not only of Biblical Christianity, but equally much of idealism itself. That is why the modern mind, which at first might have been regarded as at basal points an elongation of classic ancient convictions, involved finally the necessity of a new and different partitioning of western thought. For the modern view, in its end result, took issue with the prevailing philosophy of both ancient and medieval times; it went back, for its vital point of contact, to the suppressed naturalism of the Graeco-Roman era, which revelational Christianity had banished entirely from the medieval scene, and in spirit united with its affirmation of the ultimate reality of nature.

The transition to naturalism as the end result of modern thought was so circuitous that, at numerous intervals, naturalism was singled out as, and indeed even appeared to be for the time, the very antithesis of speculative intent. The plain fact is that the initial movements in modern philosophy were, in most regards, far nearer to Plato and Aristotle than they were to Democritus and Lucretius. No scholarly survey of the modern period can afford to slight the distinction between an idealism unable to sustain itself, and a direct attack upon the priority of mind; the former may descend finally to naturalism, but that surely is not its original intention. And modern philosophy, from its beginnings in Descartes, can hardly be regarded as intentional naturalism. Even if the early rationalistic systems passed from their source in Cartesian theism through Spinozistic pantheism, to Leibnitzian monadism, and even if Lockean empiricism passed by way of Berkleyan idealism to Humean agnosticism, the Kantian synthesis retained a salute — however grounded — to supernaturalism, and the philosophies of Fichte and Hegel and their idealistic successors have for two centuries stood out as the avowed enemy of naturalism. That at least must be said about the intention of the modern idealisms.

But idealistic thought, even if the philosophic rival of naturalistic views, erected its own highway to Marx and Nietzsche. Biblical theology had placed man at the juncture of the world of nature and spirit *in a certain way,* as a creature in sin and with hope of redemption. Naturalism placed him there in a different way: it made the supernatural a product of human imagination and desire; it denied, that is, that man stands essentially at any such juncture as Christianity affirmed at all. Now, whereas naturalism absorbed man to nature, idealism in modern times came to absorb nature and man to God or, if it tried to avoid such assimilation, it did so in such an unconvincing manner that the drift of modern thought bypassed the effort. Whereas naturalism struck at the Biblical view from the side of naturalistic monism, idealism did so from the side of spiritualistic monism; both philosophies, however extensive their differences, conspired to remove man from his Biblical status at the juncture of two realms. In overcoming the antithesis between nature and supernature not as did Plato, who regarded phenomena as effects or copies of a transcendent reality, but by making nature itself part of ultimate reality, indeed, the very thought-content of the Absolute, and then absorbing man to this thought-content, modern idealism could fix upon man's finiteness as his only distinction.

An instructive study in this connection is provided by the differences between pre-Christian and post-Christian idealism.

For post-Christian idealism had for its philosophical enemy not only naturalism but, as it soon developed, revelational theism. Put in another way, it can be said that the Biblical view which in ancient times had appeared upon the western horizon as the rescuer of certain classic emphases at a moment when the decay of idealism had set in, was now cast aside in modern times, and its vigor borrowed by a revived idealism.

Furthermore, post-Christian idealism began not with the problem of being, which was the great concern of ancient thought, but rather with the problem of knowledge. For Aristotle, clearly, epistemology served as prolegomenon to ontology. And, while Plato before him had devoted much of his energy to epistemology, it was a concern to which he was driven by the relativism of the Sophists; his later writing moves on into ontology also, so that epistemology is not made a substitute for metaphysics. In modern philosophy, however, ontology and epistemology were to be merged, so that the problem of being was frequently lost in exploring the problem of knowledge. Here what classic ancient thought had been able to take for granted, that human thought has an ontic reference, came now into dispute, with the setting aside of the medieval confidence in a divine self-revelation given historically and once-for-all. Since Christianity had made more specific and more compulsive that belief in the reality of the supernatural which classic idealism had projected as a necessity of contemplative thought, the dismissal of the Christian claim to the possession of special revelation meant that much that ancient idealism had assumed was now also to be called into question. It was not an accident of philosophy that, once the impact of revelational theism had been felt and repulsed, this occupation with the epistemological more than with the ontological should ensue, so that western thought should have to face first on almost every hand the question of what and how men know.

In another way this difference between the idealistic traditions bisected by Christianity is seen. The Biblical doctrine of sin finds no place in either the ancient or the modern idealistic tradition; the idealistic distinction between nature and the supernatural, rather than between creation and Creature, has always absorbed man's spiritual nature to the divine nature. But post-Christian idealism erected a view of man more opimistic even than that of ancient idealism. For post-Christian idealism eliminated any notion that matter and the body are evil and hence a drag on human achievement; hence it divorced itself from a certain hopelessness which characterized classic Greek thought. Rejecting the Christian emphasis that man, on his psychic side, is a sinner in revolt against God, it rejected also that the Greek emphasis that man, on his physical side, is prevented from realizing his ideals due to an evil body. In the revolt against Greek thought it was encouraged by the Christian emphasis that nature and man are a divine creation, so that matter or the body as such are not intrinsically hostile to the divine. Therefore, in rejecting the Christian view of man, modern idealism rejected also an essential aspect of the classic

Greek view of man. But it borrowed, in another regard, from that same Christianity against which it revolted. The Christian emphasis of a divine incarnation in Christ, to the intimacy of which there were no limits, became in idealism the pattern for a universal externalization of the divine in humanity at large; that conformity to the divine image which Christian theology had reserved for the state of glorification in the eschatological experience of redeemed sinners, modern idealism now made a potentiality of all men, in their natural state, who were conceived at the core of their personalities in their present relationship to God not as sinners but as intrinsically divine. Here were the outlines, of course, of the recent belief in the essential goodness of man.

This post-Christian optimism about nature and man expressed itself also in the interpretation of history. No era of human thought has seen such a production of volumes on the philosophy of history as our own. Each in its peculiar way testifies to the fact that it is through the Biblical revelation that mankind has learned to find a divine meaning in the world of historical events. The separation of the divine from history and time, as it was carried out in Greek idealism, made impossible any notion of history as the bearer of ultimate meaning. The Hebrew-Christian tradition pointed to history as the area of the divine once-for-all soteriological revelation, climaxed by the Word becoming flesh. This was a radical contrast with the Greek idealistic notion that meaning could be found only outside of history, in the changeless realm of eternal ideas. Post-Christian idealism had a very different notion, learned from Biblical theology, but formulated now in revolt against Biblical thought. For modern idealism united the divine with history and time in such a way as to underwrite the recent dogma of the inevitability of progress. The events of history were the divine activity externalized. Here the air of melancholy which hovered over the Greek view of nature and history was rejected, but that was not all. For Hebrew-Christian thought, while repudiating the chilly Greek concept of cycles of historical events without ultimate meaning, avoided at the same time any boundless optimism about history. It is true that medieval thought, after Augustine, tended to identify the Roman Catholic Church with the kingdom of God, but this was itself a profound misunderstanding of the Biblical emphasis that history, bearing divine meaning, was related to both grace and judgment, and that the kingdom would be fully inaugurated in history only in the eschatological future, at the second advent. But modern idealism went far beyond the Scholastic compromise, and issued in an unmodified optimism over history which, since it was conceived as the divine self-manifestation, could only reflect the divine in a progressive spirituality.

Post-Christian idealism was characterized therefore by an explicit revolt against special revelation, by a preoccupation with the problem of knowledge, and by an intrinsically optimistic view of men and events which concealed the reality of sin and evil. Yet, in all of this, it offered itself as the only compelling modern alternative to naturalism. This option became increasingly unconvincing to modern thought; philosophical idealism was seen to involve an inner dialectic which carried on to naturalism as its end result, and which development the coming of Christianity into the world had concealed by engendering a culture around the framework of revelational supernaturalism. At four crucial points post-Christian idealism in its major expressions had formulated its views in a way that made resistance of the naturalistic alternative difficult. These involved the nature of God, of man, of nature and of history.

By separate courses, modern idealism and naturalism obscured the reality of the supernatural, deprived man of personality and freedom, and secularized the philosophy of history. That this is so in the case of naturalism is more immediately evident than in the case of idealism. But it is not too difficult to show how idealism came to involve the same end result. Kant is the center around which modern idealism in its various expressions somehow gathers, in view of his mighty effort to bind humanity into a unity on a rationalistic basis, coupled with a positivistic view of phenomena. Within such a beginning, modern man is enmeshed more and more in nature as his environment; ultimate meaning and values gain their support from postulation, and religion, too, finds its main-stay in speculation. God ceases to be a transcendent reality, over against nature and man as His creations; rather, nature and man are "rescued" from positivism by being viewed as themselves the Absolute in manifestation. So for Hegel only the Absolute is real, and man's personality but a fleeting moment in the infinite life; the Spirit who is the subject of history is no longer human, and only ambiguously personal. Human freedom and moral responsibility were minimized, since whatever took place was somehow what the Absolute was doing.

Such a struggle against positivism, viewed from the side of Christian theology, could not be seen as other than a contribution to the very outcome that it sought to avoid, that is, as itself a slower road to naturalism. It involved already a minimizing of the individual man's spiritual significance, and an automaticizing of his relationship to the divine, and this reduction was a prelude to elimination. Kant had cut man off from rational knowledge of the noumenal, had put postulation in the place of revelation. Whatever later idealists would see in this, shrewder eyes would read it as prolegomena to future naturalism, as preparation for the anti-humanism of Marx and Nietzsche. Hegel's substitution of the divine for the human spirit as the subject of history would make possible another non-human substitution; non-personal economic factors would be the key to the course of events by the time Hegel's student, Marx, had learned the lesson of discarding the Biblical way in which man stood at the juncture of two realms. Most post-Hegelian traditions stood solidly in the pantheistic camp even when, as in the case of scholars like Andrew Seth Pringle-Pattison, or Josiah Royce, or W. E. Hocking, some effort was made to avoid the devastating implications of that view for human freedom and responsibility. For modern scholars, in ever-increasing number, there was little to choose between Hegel and Spinoza, and then little between Spinoza and Dewey. A deity so identical with the world process was too easily dismissed as only a reverent title for the process, and not in any way different from the process without benefit of such dignified terminology. It took a long time for the Renaissance, with its inheritance of a millennium of Christian conviction, to work itself free of elements which it had unconsciously absorbed and combined with its own perspective. That is why, prior to its non-Christian phase, its beginnings were rather comfortably "Christian," and also why it is not until our own times that, at long last, its anti-Christian content becomes increasingly evident. In this last movement, when the genius of naturalism reaches its terminus with considerable consistency in Nietzsche and Marx, man is only an animal of remarkable complexity.[8]

Even though recent idealism, in its personalistic trends, has sought to halt the descent of idealism to naturalism, it did not muster enough strength to forestall the rise of the mighty antipersonalisms, nor could it, for even these trends contained within them the necessity for subsequent descent.[9] The real alternatives to the discard of Biblical theism were now seen to be not a restatement of classic idealism in modern dress, in which some elements of Christianity were retained, some rejected, and most of them transformed, but rather a thorough naturalism in which every trace of Christianity, in so far as possible, would be eliminated. The genuine option was not a non-Christian metaphysics blended with a sub-Christian ethics, but an inversion which went the entire distance.

One such tack was followed by Nietzsche, with his hatred for the "herd man" — for whom Christ has died, in the supreme gesture of divine love, according to medieval theology. Nietzsche's program was to rid the earth of ordinary men, and at the same time of its reverence for the God-man, and to substitute therefore the man-God, the superman, who knows no ethics of humility, of submission, of love for enemies. Here, in Nietzsche, one could see the ripe fruit

---

8. Nicolas Berdyaev aptly observed that the Renaissance worked itself out into "an unfolding of ideas and events wherein we see humanism destroying itself by its own dialectic, for the putting up of man without God and against God, the denial of the divine image, lead to his own negation and destruction" (*The Fate of Man in the Modern World*, 29. New York: Morehouse-Gorham Company, Inc., 1935).

9. Lotze and Bowne, while they lost nature in God, placed selves outside of God, but the emphasis on moral continuity, as against the Biblical doctrine of sin and redemption, could not but obscure the significance of the human personality. In Brightman's personalism, another step is taken, and reality is explained no longer only in terms of an ultimate Self, but also in terms of an impersonal non-rational given, so that evil is explained not in terms of personal revolt, but of impersonal necessity.

which is critical mostly of secularism at a distance is a church which will lose its capacity to resist secularism at all. Evangelical Christianity will regain its prophetic vigor in our times as it learns to distinguish the kingdom of God from Capitalism and the democratic way of life, in their secularized expressions, no less than from Communism and the totalitarian way of life in its secularized expressions.

The events of our generation have been accompanied by a sweeping inversion of ideology. The drastic changes in outlook have been so often reiterated that the cultural tragedy they represent is voided of pathos. The essential goodness of man, the inevitability of progress, the ultimate reality of nature and the absolute uniformity of nature — these were cardinal tenets of the western mind a generation ago.[12] The western man has been driven, by his experience of nature and history, to some striking recantations in recent years. Why, if the world of events is ultimately natural, man should be essentially *good;* why, if progress is inevitable, man's goodness or badness would be at all relevant; why, if nature is totally uniform, there should be real *progress* — these were some of the inner difficulties of the modern eclecticism. But the outer difficulties were no less pointed. History itself disclosed a progress in warfare so destructive that by the mid-twentieth century it had brought both hemispheres into crisis, and raised for western culture the fear of the inevitability of disaster. Recent anthropology, from Freud's studies to the Nazi atrocities, and then the Russian slave camps, afforded no ground for angelicizing man. Contemporary physics, with as much of a distaste for the Biblical miraculous as philosophical rationalism, ac-

---

12. These modern dogmas are treated, in contrast with the Biblical view, in the writer's *Remaking the Modern Mind.*

knowledged discontinuities in nature, whereas the modern revolt against miracles had grown from the dogma that there could be no discontinuities. And western man, who had acted more and more for several generations on the conviction that nature is the only ultimate reality, lacking an orderly pattern of convictions, hesitated in indecision when, armed with military advantage in the superior possession of hydrogen and atomic bombs, he could have swept to victory by brute power — hesitated in indecision because somehow he felt to be real what he thought he must deny: an objective moral order, an *ought* not dictated by human expedience.

While the so-called free nations, in the leadership given them by the Anglo-Saxon lands, have suffered ideological paralysis, acting now on one motive and again on another, and not infrequently on the very ground of expedience which they so much condemned in others, Soviet Russia has taken a different course.[13] A more consistent naturalism has for the time being much more force than an idealism which does not know its own mind, more force than a naturalism which tries by virtue of sporadic elements of the ideal to keep itself from a descent to consistency. While the western nations have struggled between the alternatives of inevitable progress and inevitable despair, essential goodness and essential animality, objective and subjective morality, Russian Com-

---

13. John Foster Dulles has pointed out that "many non-Communist countries of the world, including indeed many 'Christian' nations of the West, now seem to put primary emphasis upon developing 'the material life of society' and to subordinate the spiritual development of the individual. The Communists cite that to prove that even the Western societies have had to adopt the materialistic thesis of Communism. The leaders in the West do not make any convincing denials, and the prestige of Soviet Communism in the world is greatly increased. The difficulty is that we, ourselves, are unclear as to our faith and the relationship of that faith to our practices" (*War or Peace*, 257. New York: The Macmillan Company, 1950).

munism has not been double-minded. The denial of God is
the first Russian commandment; nature is ultimate, that is
the first principle of dialectical materialism.[14] Moral distinctions are subjective and arbitrary; there is no changeless moral order.[15] If and when it is expedient to do so,

---

14. Marx and Engels, in their *Manifesto of the Communist Party*
(1848) emphasized that "law, morality, religion, are to him (i. e., the
proletarian) so many bourgeois prejudices, behind which lurk in ambush
just as many bourgeois interests" (*ibid.*, 28. Chicago: Charles H. Kerr
& Company, 1947), and that "man's ideas, views and conceptions, in
one word, man's consciousness, changes with every change in the
condition of his material existence, in his social relations and in his
social life" (*ibid.*, 40). Joseph Stalin, who collaborated closely with
the authors of the *History of the Communist Party of the Soviet Union,*
wrote personally a section for the fourth chapter, on "Dialectical and
Historical Materialism." In it, he labors the material rather than the
spiritual basis of the universe, as Marx conceived it. He rejects not
only the idealistic view that nature is mental, but also what is common
to Christianity and idealism, the primacy of the spiritual: "The Marxist
materialist philosophy holds that... matter is primary... and that mind
is secondary, derivative, since it is a reflection of matter which in its
development has reached a high degree of perfection, namely, of
the brain, and the brain is the organ of thought; and that therefore
one cannot separate thought from matter without committing a grave
error" (Stalin, *Dialectical and Historical Materialism,* 15f. New York:
International Publishers, 1940).

15. "The practical activity of the party of the proletariat," wrote
Stalin, "must not be based on... 'universal morals,' etc., but on the laws
of development of society and on the study of these laws" (*ibid.*, 19).
The same relativism is apparent in the following quotation which,
while it has in view specifically politico-economic ideologies, reflects
the broader revolt against eternal and objective truth and morality:
"If the world is in a state of constant movement and development, if
the dying away of the old and the upgrowth of the new is a law of
development, then it is clear that there can be no 'immutable' social
systems, no 'eternal principles' of private property and exploitation, no
'eternal ideas' of the subjugation of the peasant to the landlord, of the
worker to the capitalist (Stalin, *Dialectical and Historical Materialism,*
13. New York: International Publishers, 1940). Stalin also writes that
"every social movement in history must be evaluated not from the
standpoint of 'eternal justice'... but from the standpoint of the conditions which gave rise to that system or that social movement..."
(*ibid.*, 12).

Russia will use atomic weapons; no unarticulated flirtation with the possibility of an objective moral *ought*, but rather an uncompromised policy of expedience, will decide the issue. Not only has Russia appropriated the naturalism to which the philosophy of western culture, cut loose from Christian moorings, has gravitated, but she has retained as a cardinal concept what the Anglo-Saxon nations tend increasingly to discard: the inevitability of progress. The shadow of pessimism which has gathered over the thought patterns of the West is counterbalanced by the cloud of optimism in the East: the inevitability of the triumph of the communistic cause. Marx and Engels had written, concerning the bourgeois class, that "its fall and the victory of the proletariat are equally inevitable."[16] and this text is to the party workers what the Great Commission was to the Christian movement in its infancy.

In this communistic version of naturalism, the spiritual life of man is completely submerged and human personality reduced to an impersonal dimension in a sense in which it is absent in secularized Capitalism except in its most radical expressions. For, as Joseph Stalin himself has reiterated, the thesis that the material world is primary and the mental and spiritual world secondary, carried with it a certain view of society; "it follows," wrote Stalin, "that the material life of society, its being, is also primary, and its spiritual life secondary, derivative, and that the material life of society is an objective reality existing independently of the will of men, while the spiritual life of society is a reflection of this objective reality, a reflection of being."[17] The social order

---

16. Marx and Engels, *ibid.*, 30.
17. Stalin, *ibid.*, 20.

determines men's consciousness, not men's consciousness the social order, on this approach. The conditions of the life of society turn out to be, therefore, material and impersonal, and basically economic, on the communist appraisal.

Communism has found its alternative, therefore, to the western world's discard of the essential goodness of man, the inevitability of progress, the unquestioned ultimacy of nature. It is the essential animality of man, the inevitability of the triumph of the Marxist cause, the primacy of the material and the peripheral significance of the spiritual and moral. Here we begin to see the meaning of a pure naturalism. What it means, to affirm that nature is the primal reality, was perhaps clearer to ancient naturalists than to post-Christian naturalists, because all subsequent traditions have imbibed something of the spirit of the Biblical view. Naturalism, no less than idealism, has its debt to the Hebrew-Christian tradition, which has modified both in a manner of which sponsors of those views are frequently quite unaware. It might be contended, of course, that ancient naturalism was naive, and that modern naturalism is quite ready to embrace corrective elements which may be required for an adequate view of reality, but the question must be asked nonetheless whether modern naturalism has not undergone a certain romanticizing. The naturalistic thesis, that nature is the ultimate real, and furnishes the proper point of reference for all that exists, meant in ancient times the relativity of knowledge, the intrinsic animality of man, and the subjectivity of morals. A world in which change is the last word is a world in which changeless gods, future immortality, and an abiding goodness and truth are alien inhabitants — except, of course, as mythological postulations of fancy. That the concept of deity is simply an intense form of the projection of a temporary ideal, that man is simply a more complex animal than his fellow creatures, that morality is simply the culture pattern approved by the creaturely environment in which one lives — these have been central affirmations also of the distinctively recent world view. Theology, anthropology and morality alike undergo a staggering transformation on the naturalistic approach, with its eliminating of the supernatural, and its redefinition of God and man and the true and the good in terms of the changing movements of nature alone.

Nothing is more striking than the way in which communist leaders appeal to modern science in support of their veiws. Quite in Lenin's spirit, Stalin has championed scientific knowledge of the laws of nature not alone as the only truth which men possess, but as "objective truth" which replaces the "eternal truth" of the supernaturalistic traditions. Moreover, especially in the interest of the naturalistic view of man and society Stalin appeals to modern science. Thus we are told that "the data of science regarding the laws of development of society are authentic data having the validity of objective truths. Hence the science of the history of society, despite all the complexity of the phenomena of social life, can become as precise a science as. . .biology, and capable of making use of the laws of development of society for practical purposes."[18] These laws then turn out to be impersonal economic factors.

What is clear in all of this is that the naturalistic view, in our times, has gained a clear victory. It has become the con-

18. Stalin, *ibid.*, 19f.

scious framework of the mighty Soviet, and it has robbed the
idealism of the free nations of vitality. Naturalism, definite
or indefinite, hovers as the central issue on the horizon of
world decision today. It is a more important issue by far,
what the twentieth century man is to do with deity and morality, than what he is do with his property; to make private
property the supreme issue of our age, whether one ranges
himself on the capitalist or communist side, is already to act
on the naturalistic thesis that our problems are basically eco-
nomical. It is by no means clear that, simply because he
opposes private property, a man cannot be a believer in objective morality, and more specifically in Biblical redemption; any more than it follows that, simply because a man
is a capitalist, he is bound for kingdom come. What is basically at stake in our times is the issue of the reality of the
supernatural, the issue of the acceptance or rejection of the
God who has spoken in Jesus Christ and the Scriptures.
When once that is seen to be the basic issue, men are no
longer divided primarily as communists or capitalists, but
as believers and unbelievers, which the Bible affords us every
encouragement to assume is after all the really durable distinction.

That modern science leaves no alternative to a naturalistic
view of man and the world is not a thesis made in Russia;
American thinkers have affirmed it with a vigor not outdone
abroad.   John Dewey furnishes an excellent example of this
temper which, in the name of science, repudiates supernaturalism as an obstacle on the highway of progressive thought.
His *The Quest for Certainty*, remarkably enough a series
of Gifford lectures, designated the scientific method as the
only avenue to truth, and on the ground of the modern

scientific world view repudiated any notion of an antecedent deity in whom perfection is realized as an actuality.[19] Similarly, Harry Elmer Barnes, in *The Twilight of Christianity,* outmoded not only ancient and medieval supernaturalism, but modern religious liberalism, on the ground of "the astonishing scientific progress of the twentieth century.[20] Almost in the same paragraph we read of "the development and validity of the scientific explanation of religion offered by psychology, anthropology and sociology," and that "the personification of the cosmic God is, of course, a product of wishful thinking and anthropocentric formulations.[21] John Herman Randall Jr. provides a third representative illustration, championing the modern "faith in the efficacy of the methods of experimental intelligence"[22] and declaring bluntly that "the modern world takes what *nature* offers it, and builds a structure in which it may hope to find en-

19. "I shall try to show," wrote Dewey, "how modern philosophies, in spite of their great diversity, have been concerned with problems of adjustment of the conclusions of modern science to the chief religious and moral tradition of the western world" (*The Quest for Certainty,* 29. New York: Minton, Balch & Co., 1929). "According to the religious and philosophic tradition of Europe, the valid status of all the highest values... was bound up with their being properties of ultimate and supreme Being... All went well as long as what passed for natural science gave no offence to this conception. Trouble began when science ceased to disclose in the objects of knowledge the possession of any such properties. Then some roundabout method had to be devised for substantiating them" (42f.).

20. Barnes affirmed that an attitude favorable to the Christian Epic in any form is due to ignorance "of the advances in psychology and the social sciences and their application to religion" (*The Twilight of Christianity,* 331. New York: The Vanguard Press, 1929). We are told that "science is as yet unable either to prove or disprove the existence of God" (*ibid.,* 332), the undisputed premise being that science is the sole arbiter of the issue.

21. *Ibid.,* 333.

22. John Herman Randall Jr., *The Making of the Modern Mind,* 679. (Boston: Houghton Miffllin Company, 1940).

joyment and power."[23]   Whatever may be the differences between contemporary naturalists, the thesis which they maintain in common is that modern science requires a sharp rupture with the idealisms and supernaturalisms of the past, and that a maturing to the empirical discoveries of our times demands the erection of a naturalistic alternative.

This conviction has been pressed with such vigor during the past fifty years that western philosophy has witnessed a shrinkage in the prestige of the idealisms and a coming to power by the naturalisms.   Centers of academic study and propaganda either passed to naturalistic control or, in instance after instance, idealism was compromised or neutralized as an effective philosophical alternative.   The naturalistic assault on the traditional view of man and morality was made in such force that a whole generation has now come to maturity which, while it may not in the Anglo-Saxon democratic lands be fully committed to the naturalistic bias, nonetheless does not resist it vigorously from an idealistic or theistic perspective, because the modern philosophical statements seemed unconvincing to a majority. The infiltration of the western mind by naturalistic relativism has coincided with the current cultural collapse and, to a considerable degree, contributed both indirectly and directly to it.   A culture lacking a conviction that any goal whatever *ought* to be pursued permanently, and without any single unifying objective in its academic life, and dedicated progressively to the elimination[24] of the "fetish" of changeless norms and the substitution therefore of temporary ideals

---

23. *Ibid.*, 616, italics supplied.

24. Dogmatic naturalism which refuses to go its proper course to skepticism, has its own "fetish": the unchanging dogma that all norms are changing and provisional.

which are somehow obligatory for us, has already imbibed the hemlock of death.

That the necessity for naturalism derives from modern science is, of course, an insincere claim; naturalism existed before modern science, and modern science is compatible with the full rejection of naturalism.[25] Certain influential philosophies of science are naturalistic, but that is very far from saying that science requires naturalism; equally intricate philosophies of science are idealistic. Among the ablest Gifford lecturers must be ranged many contemporary minds, some of them with an impressive background in one or another of the modern sciences, who have cast their weight for a supernaturalistic view.[26] Moreover, able scientists maintain memberships still in orthodox churches, and do so by a sense of spiritual conviction and decision.[27] The fre-

25. C. E. M. Joad has written that "so far as English and American scientists are concerned, the leaders seem almost unanimously to disown any exclusive claim on the part of science to give us information about the nature of reality" (*Philosophical Aspects of Modern Science*, 189. London: George Allen & Unwin, 1932). In this regard, the dogmatism of a half century ago has been tempered no little in scientific circles. But scientists who are "open" to values and the supernatural, but who never find a positive basis for belief in these, are hardly a deterrent to naturalism.

26. The Gifford Lectures, in the provision which Lord Gifford made for them, encourage a positive view of natural theology which Reformation Protestantism would hardly have endorsed. This works itself out in remarkably competitive ways; one need think only of James Ward, C. Lloyd Morgan, W. R. Sorley, and A. E. Taylor as examples. In recent years, however, even neosupernaturalistic thinkers like Barth and Brunner have been included.

27. The recent compilation by American men of science who hold Protestant evangelical convictions, titled *Modern Science and Christian Faith*, (Wheaton, Ill.: Van Kampen Press, 1948) is a significant even if popular work. It is a reminder that scientists who declare that science requires them to be naturalists actually lend the prestige of their profession to a philosophy which it does not require, that it is not on the basis of what one learns by the so-called scientific method that he decides the issue for or against supernaturalism.

quently voiced sentiment that modern science requires naturalism is an unscientific boast; science requires nothing of the sort.

Science — in the modern sense[28] of phenomenal knowledge gained by sensual means, requiring laboratory verification and subject to constant revision — is impotent to decide the issue of the reality or unreality of the supernatural.

Alongside the question whether modern science requires naturalism stands a related question, whether the knowledge which modern science affords is such that, when thought through, it really supersedes the melancholy relativism which in pre-scientific days was regarded as the consistent implication of naturalism. Modern science has infused naturalism with a certain optimism which it did not possess in ancient times, because it has held out the hope of control of nature, witnessed in the tremendous successes of applied science. The naturalistic thesis, in ancient times, involved a rather hopeless and melancholy attitude toward life. Man is a creature only of time and change; since nature is the ultimate, he has no genuine tie to an eternal changeless realm no hope of immortality. On top of that, the shortness and uncertainty of life plague him. Hence his great problem is the maximal satisfaction of his egoistic desires in such a way as not to hasten death, nor yet to be overtaken by it prematurely in terms of such satisfactions. Now, the skill of modern science has doubtless added many years to the life

28. This is, of course, an arbitrary restriction of the meaning of the word, which is properly used of all systematized and correlated knowledge. In this broader sense the ancients could speak of science of philosophy, and the medievals of the science of theology. The modern restriction of the word, significantly, already assumes that only what is known by empirical methodology under laboratory conditions is worthy of being dignified as systematized knowledge — which is the very thing under dispute! The revolt against all absolutes issues in the absolutizing of the scientific method.

of infants and children and adults who fell prey in earlier
ages to dread sickness and disease, but it has also imple-
mented many ways for sudden and mass death through its
technological advances, whether in peace-time industry or
in warfare. It requires a considerable epidemic of childhood
diseases to rival the destructive power of a hydrogen bomb
which can cover twelve hundred square miles so as to cancel out a concentration of fifty armed divisions and their
equipment. With regard to neither the survival of man beyond physical death, nor the lengthening of man's days beyond that always attributable to the human species by the
elimination of the certainty of death, nor by substantially
eradicating the uncertainty of death, has modern science
made any striking difference. So that those areas which,
within a naturalistic frame, seemed to ancient thinkers to
rob life of its optimism, remain substantially unaltered by
modern science. Moreover, in its production of the atomic
and hydrogen bombs, it has confronted secularized humanity
with its greatest potential for pessimism in the modern era,
unless some guarantee be found that these will be devoted
only to peaceful pursuits. But precisely due to a naturalistic
mood the modern danger of mass destruction confronts humanity in our times as an everpresent possibility.

The world can be rescued from despair in our era not
by the opposition of tender-hearted American naturalism to
tough-minded Soviet naturalism, not by the opposition of
benevolent sentimental idealism to humanism nor to an ethics
of sheer power, but only by humble repentance and submission of multitudes of men and women to the speaking God,
who has not stuttered in His speech. The lines of hatred
which today separate East and West are as momentous as

any to be found in the known history of man.   Never since the followers of Jesus Christ first ventured forth into a world in the shackles of paganism has the Christian revelation-claim confronted humanity with such urgency for study. Philosophical idealism may have restrained and minimized naturalism in ancient times, before naturalism could gain an appeal because of an illegitimate blending with elements absorbed surreptitiously from Christianity, but post-Christian naturalism, armed with the achievements of the scientific method and, more important, with a comprehensive naturalistic philosophy which turned them to its own advantage, could be met only by a supernaturalism which found its vitality not in philosophical postulation, but in the self-revealing God who speaks not merely through philosophers with gifted insight but who has spoken on His own account, both by Word and in history, in such a way as to confront naturalism itself with judgment.

THE CHRISTIAN REVELATION-CLAIM

III

The Christian Revelation-Claim

MUCH more is seen to turn, this mid-twentieth century, upon the reception or discard of the Christian view of things, than has been obvious heretofore. The question comes constantly to the surface, whether the idealistic ideologies of the West can maintain themselves against strictly humanistic views, especially against the dialectical naturalism stemming from the Russian states, once the validity of the Christian view is set aside. It cannot much be doubted that the idealistic philosophies which thrived during a century of competition with revelational theism, in the wake of the magnetic influence of Kant, Hegel and Lotze, have been unable in the final test to sustain a convincing case for a supernaturalistic world view. Their half century of prestige, in which the speculative idealisms offered to the modern mind an appealing synthesis of theological, philosophical and scientific thought, subsequently gave way to another half century in which they have had to struggle increasingly for survival. The bold contention of Nietzsche, quite unheeded by the multitudes in his day, that not idealism but naturalism is the legitimate alternative to the discard of the Biblical outlook, is now sensed to possess more radical realism than once was granted. If the acceptance of Biblical theism must involve a major revision of the prevailing modern outlook, its consistent rejection is now seen to require, for western culture, vaster changes than those which earlier generations perceived.

Divorced from the Biblical appeal to miraculous revelation, contemporary idealism was unable permanently to engender in modern culture those great convictions which, in ancient Greek times, Socrates and Plato and Aristotle had welded at the hub of the classical outlook: the reality of an unchanging spiritual order, the superanimality of man, and the objectivity of morals. Graeco-Roman culture, although possessing such idealistic convictions, lacked the moral dynamic to escape declension and doom. But the cultural collapse did not mean, in those times, the displacement of supernaturalism by naturalism.

For Biblical Christianity lifted the ancient world out of the rubbles of paganism. That great historical fact was too superficially overlooked by modern thinkers. And the easy dismissal of Biblical Christianity by those who felt that a theistic view of things could be maintained compellingly on other grounds soon took its toll; the movement from René Descartes to John Dewey issued in the dissolution of western culture and the dominance of that materialistic perspective which in ancient times had come only to minority expression. A culture which today lacks the vitality to propel itself from naturalism to a compelling idealism of any species might well meditate at some length on the dynamic with which Christianity challenged a world unable to fulfill its idealistic longings.

The modern man is confronted, therefore, with a broader choice than in any previous era of history, simply because naturalism is today a central issue. The options are no longer, as they seemed to be in classic Greek times, philosophical idealism or naturalism, nor as they seemed three centuries ago, revelational theism or philosophical theism, but rather more obviously than at any time in the history of serious speculative thought, the final choice when once the illegitimate intermediates are removed is between Biblical theology and nihilism. The prime problem is whether naturalism can be avoided consistently, not whether it is possible for the time being to establish a spurious midway preventative. A careful study of the history of philosophy will disclose that all the significant stopping-points between these alternatives have been ventured upon and have issued, because of inherent impossibilities, in modification and compromise which, sooner or later, resulted in yet further movement. The genuine alternates are the Biblical revelation or a naturalistic emptying of the meaning of life and the voiding of the significance of history.

If therefore the meaning which Christianity inserts into life and the significance which it ascribes to human events calls the modern man to the task of searching inquiry, there can be no excuse today for evading it. The times are apocalyptic on any reading; the era has come when date-fixing for the final cataclysmic summons has proceeded not from impassioned evangelists, but from emotionless scientists. The signs of crisis dot every realm of human endeavor; theology, philosophy, sociology, economics, and the physical sciences as well are involved in revolutionary change. A world of unrelieved change, of perpetual motion unabsorbed to a context of meaning, is reduced to unintelligibility. The modern man, simply to save significance for himself, is driven in his extremity to a final resurrection of the problem of ultimates.

Christianity, as already indicated, proclaims itself to be a revelational view of God and the world, and, as such, a view of perpetual significance.[1] It is clear, of course, that the concepts of deity and revelation belong together, so that the question of divine manifestation is in the forefront of all genuinely religious inquiry. The belief in a god or gods about whom nothing at all can be known has always eked out an embarrassed survival in intellectual circles, simply because those who speak at length about such gods do so after initially denying themselves the right to any certainty of their existence. The religious history of mankind is, in a real sense, revelation history; the smoking altars and crowded temples reflect man's refusal to dismiss the idea of God as something simply of his own making. Any view of God affirmed to be final and absolute, by way of appeal to special revelation, must somehow bring within its perspective the sum of the spiritual yearnings of all mankind, presupposing as these do the existence of a religious object upon which man is dependent. The term "revelation" covers more territory than a single stream of world history, even if the Hebrew-Christian events have come to serve as the center of religious interest. Christianity, if it is to make good its claim to universal and perpetual significance, must relate itself to the other views of God and the world. And this it does not

---

1. James Orr concluded his famous Kerr Lectures appropriately: "I do not.... believe that the Christian view is obsolete; that it is doomed to go down like a faded constellation in the west of the sky of humanity. I do not believe that, in order to preserve it, one single truth we have been accustomed to see shining in that constellation will require to be withdrawn... The world needs them all, and will one day acknowledge it. It is not with a sense of failure, therefore, but with a sense of triumph, that I see the progress of the battle between faith and unbelief. I have no fear that the conflict will issue in defeat. Like the ark above the waters, Christ's religion will ride in safety the waves of present-day unbelief, as it has ridden the waves of unbelief in days gone by, bearing in it the hopes of the future of humanity" (*The Christian View of God and the World*, 347. New York: Charles Scribner's Sons, 1897).

hesitate to do; in fact, Christianity involves a specific view of the non-Christian religions. Christianity, by its claim to be the one true religion, does not imply that God has left Himself everywhere else without a witness. The apostle Paul, in his sweeping indictment of the pagan religions, at the same time plainly affirmed, to quote Calvin, "that God has presented to the minds of all the means of knowing him, having so manifested himself by his works, that they must necessarily see what of themselves they seek not to know — that there is some God."[2] Christianity does not deny that God is everywhere revealed in the space-time universe, and internally in the very mind and conscience of man as well. The actual revelation of God in nature, history and man is a central Biblical affirmation. Elmer A. Leslie has fitly written of "the perpetual anthem of the heavens;"[3] R. C. H. Lenski has emphasized that whatever the distortion of man's moral sense, there remains divinely written upon human hearts a witness to God in which the conscience and mind participate.[4] That there is a universal and continuing divine revelation is a fundamental Biblical insistence. In view of this revelation, human history is history conditioned inescapably by a relationship to God.

---

2. John Calvin, *Commentaries on the Epistle of Paul the Apostle to the Romans,* 71 (Grand Rapids: Wm B. Eerdmans Pub. Co., 1947), on Romans 1:21: "Because that, when they knew God, they glorified him not as God, neither were thankful; but became vain in their imaginations, and their foolish heart was darkened."

3. Elmer A. Leslie, *The Psalms,* 134 (New York: Abingdon-Cokesbury Press, 1949), where he translates Psalm 19:1 as follows: "The heavens keep recounting the glory of God, and the firmament keeps declaring the work of His hand."

4. R. C. H. Lenski, *The Interpretation of St. Paul's Epistle to the Romans,* 164ff. (Columbus: The Wartburg Press, 1945), on Romans 2:15.

But Hebrew-Christian revelation interprets man's relationship in terms of man's spiritual rebellion; and conveys as the essence of religion, the special revelation and redemption of God consequent upon the sinful revolt of man. The non-Christian religions affirm gods on terms of fellowship with man in his present spiritual and moral condition; Christianity, by its proclamation of the necessity of a divinely provided salvation stamps those religions as false which conceal or misrepresent the need and way of salvation. Christianity denies that human religious history has followed an upward course of increasing approximation to God; rather, it declares that man's story is one of rebellion, of the fashioning of competitive gods in whose presence man can live the lie of acceptability.[5] That man is not on congenial and fraternal terms with the holy Creator and Lord, rather, is implicated not alone in Adamic revolt, but in rebellion against God on his own account also, is a first principle of Biblical theology. Modern philosophies and theologies have deadened such emphases as man's sin and God's wrath; they have tended to reduce the disturbing discontinuity between the holy Lord and rebellious creatures to a minor squabble or a wrangle without implications for all humanity. That is why it is particularly necessary not to obscure what Biblical theology so clearly states about man: that he is a lost sinner, in a state of rebellion against God, doomed by his dis-

---

5. Sir William Ramsay indicted the modern view that primitive religion is degraded and contemporary religion elevated, and accepted the Biblical view that the movement of the religions outside the sphere of special revelation has been downward: "My experience and reading show nothing to confirm the modern assumptions in religious history, and a great deal to confirm Paul. Wherever evidence exists, with the rarest exceptions, the history of religion among men is a history of degeneration" (*The Cities of St. Paul*, 17. Grand Rapids: Baker Book House, 1949).

obedience to continual separation from the Lord of history, and unable from his side to satisfy the demands of infinite righteousness. A sinner under divine wrath, his projection of gods galore, which makes the true God out to be something less than the holy God against whom he is in rebellion, or makes Him out to be a chatty god privately assuring every rebel that He does not take sin seriously or that He regards as perfect everybody who does the best that he or she can under the circumstances — as if anybody always does! — simply furnishes another evidence of the depth of human sin. Man is a lost sinner; whoever does not understand that, misunderstands the Christian declaration of God's special saving revelation.

The objection to the possibility of special revelation reached its zenith with the outworking of modern philosophy in the naturalistic direction. Just as the concept of the miraculous was held by the moderns to involve an orderless universe in which all scientific regularity must be abandoned[6] — despite the fact that it was the Christian rationale of nature which furnished the impetus to the rise of western science — so too the concept of special revelation has been held to be an unpermitted appeal, supposedly involving the sacrifice of intelligibility and coherence. But this is a specious sort of *apriorism*, condemned by the history of philosophy itself. For the division of the history of philosophy into three periods — ancient, medieval and modern — is not an accidental division, whatever elements of subjectivity may

6. See, for example, Charles E. Raven, *Science, Religion and the Future*, 22 (New York: The Macmillian Company, 1944).

have entered into it.[7] One of the most striking turns in the whole movement of philosophic thought — and one which the modern mind has least called attention to — occurs at the commencement of medieval philosophy. The cardinal problem which occupied the philosophers of the middle ages was not "is there a special divine revelation?" but rather, *how is special revelation related to reason?* The question did not concern the *possibility* of special revelation; the coming of Jesus Christ into the world had settled that.[8] The medieval philosophers began with the *actuality* of special divine revelation, and they did so not merely as a philosophic first principle but in terms of a remarkable crisis in history. They had matured to two great facts: the collapse of Graeco-Roman culture despite the classic idealism around which it was built; the lifting of the world from the despair of pa-

7. I am not referring to the modern tendencies to regard all supernaturalisms as essentially alike, so that the distinction between ancient classic idealism and medieval supernaturalism is blurred, or to regard all philosophic perspectives as necessarily temporary, so that any view can be dated as modern only presumptuously, although such objections are sometimes heard. But I refer to the fact that, from the Christian perspective, the Renaissance mood quite arbitrarily bracketed the Biblical view of things as an "in between" view belonging to the "middle" ages, and assumed something of the claim to finality, against which it was presumably in revolt, for itself. From the Biblical vantage point, Christianity is hardly an "in between" view, but covers the whole of history; it embraces the creation, the story of man, and the consummation of history. Yet the "eternal view," or Biblical theology, is hardly reducible to medieval Christianity; from the Biblical perspective, the Roman Catholic compromises of Christianity must also be dated as "in between" — but here it is Biblical supernaturalism that stands in judgment.

8. "Being and Becoming were the problems of ancient philosophy at its beginning: the conceptions with which it closes are God and the human race," wrote W. Windelband, *A History of Philosophy*, 262 (New York: Macmillan and Co., 1893). "There is perhaps no better proof of the power of the impression which the personality of *Jesus of Nazareth* had left," he continued, "than the fact that all doctrines of Christianity. . . are. . .at one in seeking in him and his appearance the *centre of the world's history*" (256).

ganism by the Hebrew-Christian message. Thus the coming of Jesus Christ into the world left a mark not only upon Jerusalem, but also upon Athens. For the philosophers now pursued their persistent problems within two far-reaching assumptions: (1) the reality of special revelation, and (2) its relationship to reason, or to general revelation.

If a reply is now made to the objections which have been urged against the possibility of special revelation, it is not thereby implied that the probability of such a particular divine disclosure could have been demonstrated antecedently to its actual communication.[9] For the Biblical disclosure of divine salvation is declared by itself to be the free, gracious provision of the God of holy love; there is nowhere any intimation that sinful humanity could lay claim to God's propitiatory forgiveness. The special revelation of God's redemptive mercy, the promise of divine redemption to be fulfiled in the sending of God's only-begotten Son, the free promise of the unobligated Lord, could not be known in advance, for the only proper expectation on the part of the sinner, is the necessity for the complete satisfaction of divine righteousness. That such satisfaction is provided in the gift of God's Son, by the Saviour, is the "good tidings" at the very heart of the Biblical message. But the "defense" of the concept of special or particular historical revelation proceeds today, as it proceeded initially, not from the side of the likely

9. Augustus Hopkins Strong raised more problems than he solved when he incorporated a section on *a priori* reasons for expecting a special revelation from God (*Lectures on Theology*, 31. Rochester: Press of E. R. Andrews, 1876), for the argument requires him to interpret the knowledge of man as sinner more positively than is justified, and to minimize the significance of God's election love in historical revelation. This high view of general religion as a preparation for Christianity was clearly more compatible with the philosophy of ethical monism, which Strong came to espouse, than with an uncompromised Biblical theology.

anticipation of such divine disclosure, but rather from the side of its actuality.

Nevertheless Christianity welcomes the honest inquiry of the doubter, for it fears nothing from investigation. The movement of Christian apologetics has repeatedly demonstrated that, when skeptics have come in the spirit of unbiased cross-examination, they have learned much about the nature of their concealed prepossessions in the process of exposure to the case for Christian theism. Christianity has far less to gain from that dogmatic pre-judgment of unbelievers who refuse even to probe contrary possibilities, than from a spirit which, while perhaps unconvinced, is theoretically open to the claim of a maximally coherent view of things.

The fact is, Christianity has needed constantly to justify to itself the Hebrew-Christian claim to special Biblical revelation. It is possible, of course, for a supernaturalistic bias, no less than for a naturalistic bias, to be inherited uncritically. But the drift of western thought has been such that it makes it more difficult for men to be believers than unbelievers. Apart from the fact that each generation must make its own ideological choices, since the past cannot guarantee the present in this regard, it requires far more in the way of spiritual decision to stand today on the side of the Christian revelation of man as sinner redeemed by the God of holy love. There is a sense in which the intelligent Christian believer alone has plumbed most deeply the doubts about the very existence of special revelation, for he most fully understands the Christian claim from its own side, and is thus able to expose it to a maximal test. Driven to evaluate the objections to his view with a life-and-death earnestness, perhaps the Christian believer is the ablest doubter.

Surely the believer is not unaware of the reproaches against the Hebrew-Christian revelation-claim: that it is simply one of many such claims, as witness Mohammedanism in the Orient or Mormonism in America; that it involves the necessity for additional revelation, since conservative and liberal theologians disagree widely as to what constitutes the essence of Christianity, and where this is granted Calvinistic and Arminian theologians give competitive statements of the Biblical perspective, while pulpiteers in the various denominations proclaim with equal dogmatism competitive interpretations of the same Scripture passages. Where the doubts of the world are put aside, the Christian must still vindicate to himself his faith in the Redeemer-God who manifests Himself in a particular manner.

The fact is that, granted competitive revelation-claims, granted disagreement over the central elements of the Christian claim, and granted the conflict of views over the meaning of particular texts or a given element within the whole, the existence of a special revelation might *still* be a reality. The actuality of a special revelation is not dependent upon whether everyone receives it, nor even upon whether the great majority of men receive it — especially not when the revelation itself entertains no such expectation about itself — but exclusively upon the question whether God has revealed Himself in such a way or not. Indeed, Christianity has been embarrassed not alone because later religious viewpoints like Mohammedanism and Mormonism have borrowed its principle of special revelation for alien outlooks, but even more so because the vitality of special revelation has been transferred by advocates of Biblical theism to man-made interpretations both in theology and science, which were not, by any fair exegesis, derivable from the Scriptures themselves. The Roman Catholic record of the espousal of false absolutes which were enforced by persecution made its contribution to the despite for all absolutistic claims. The confession that systematic theologies are not, any more than systematic theologians, infallible, would do much to shed light upon the variant statements of Biblical revelation. Neither the competing interpretations of the Christian revelation-claim, nor the existence of competing revelation-claims on the part of other religions,[10] would constitute a disproof of the actuality of special revelation. Assuredly, any view which makes the revelation-claim will need to account for the presence of alternative claims, and for their compelling hold upon the minds of large members of men, as well as for the misconstructions of its own claim. But the question whether, indeed, there exists a genuine once-for-all disclosure must certainly be determined by the divine activity in relation to men and nothing else.

The objections to special Biblical revelation, formulated by the modern mind, fall into four categories. They derive

10. The assumption that the Hebrew-Christian revelation-claim has many parallels is gratuitous, and grows out of the modern suspicion of all supernaturalism. What is distinctive about Biblical revelation is its express denial that it is the "highest" expression of general religion — its refusal to make a claim like that of Buddhism, or of any of the pantheistic religions, that all religions are developments, in various degrees of a universal essence, which comes to "maximal" manifestation in this one particular stand. Christianity claims to a once-for-all historical revelation, and hence not a higher variety of a general disclosure; it professes to be a "saving" revelation for mankind in revolt against a general revelation. Those religious pantheisms of the Orient, stressing a radical universal divine immanence at the expense of divine transcendence, cannot accommodate anything like a once-for-all revelation, but only a "higher" or a "lower" form of a disclosure found everywhere. Moreover, Biblical revelation requires a personal, sovereign, holy, gracious God who, as Creator and Lord, guides the destinies of men and nations by His control of history. That is, Biblical revelation is not a species of divine disclosure for which a parallel can be found appended to almost any sort of God-concept; it requires the Biblical God.

from philosophies which affirm either the supposed *impossibility,* or *superfluity,* or *immorality,* or *bigotry,* of special revelation. It is now necessary to consider these criticisms of the concept of particularism in divine disclosure.

1. The *impossibility* of special revelation is urged not only by naturalists who deny the very existence of the supernatural but by many who, while admitting the reality of the supernatural, hold that all truth must be arrived at by the empirical method, and hence is tentative or relative in nature. The essence of this view is the denial of absolute truth — a position which is underwritten in modern times especially by humanists and by logical positivists, as in ancient times it was underwritten by the Greek sophists. The notion that human knowledge is fashioned exclusively within the net of empirical observation and experiment, and therefore must be characterized by that tentativity or relativity characteristic of all such scientific inference, has fastened itself upon the modern mind with extraordinary intensity.[11] No openings are permitted in the seamless net of empirical probabilities; absolutes are identified with ancient mythologies or medieval superstitions unworthy of the enlightened modern mind.[12]

11. Emil Brunner has remarked that "the most characteristic element of the present age. . .which distinguishes it from earlier periods in history, is the almost complete disappearance of the sense of transcendence and the consciousness of revelation" (*Revelation and Reason,* 4. Philadelphia: The Westminster Press, 1946).

12. It never seems to occur to Harry Elmer Barnes, for example, that what he dismisses as "the primitive view of the direct interference of God in human affairs" may reflect more truth about the supernatural than the modern reduction of God to nature, which is at the heart of Barnes' plea for "a modernized view of religion which takes the methods and facts of science as its point of departure" (*The Twilight of Christianity,* 346, 367. New York: The Vanguard Press, 1929). Christian thinkers will insist, of course, that justice be done to assured scientific

It is true, of course, that the dogmatism of this position is tempered by suggestions of the *improbability* rather than the *impossibility,* of special revelation — a variant found not, for apparent reasons, among naturalists who deny the reality of the supernatural, but rather among those who, while not denying the supernatural, are agnostic rather than gnostic concerning it. It may be that, when the more moderated claim is investigated, it will be seen to rest upon presuppositions which are identical with those on which the assertion of the impossibility, rather than mere improbability, of such revelation rests, but the softer statement, at any rate entrenches the skeptic behind a barricade which requires a somewhat more thorough attack. Nonetheless, whether improbability or impossibility is asserted on the ground that all knowledge is experimental and subject to revision, in the end, the same exclusion of a revelational absolute is intended. According to the supporters of this anti-revelational bias, the appeal to special divine disclosure necessitates too radical a rupture with the fruitful empirical method, moving as it does from the known to the unknown, from man and his experience to God and His activity, to win the confidence of the modern mind.

And it must not be denied that Christianity, like every world religion, has much to learn from modern experimental science. The hostility of some medieval theologians in the

facts, but what Barnes asks is that violence be done to the data of religion: "Religions have invariably been the product of human ignorance, and such wisdom as exists in religious beliefs and theological concepts is nothing but the sagacity of man" (*Ibid.,* 118). Here the words *invariably* and *nothing but* display the absolutism of a contemporary empiricist. The dismissal of revelational religion grows out of the presumption that only those realities exist which are known by the tools of empirical science: "Religion can at best only hope to generalize upon the basis of the facts which have already been discovered by science" (*Ibid.,* 364).

name of Christian faith to the Copernican view of the universe, for example was never able to justify itself in terms of any Biblical insistence that the spiritual centrality of the earth depended, according to divine revelation, upon its physical or astronomical centrality. Strangely enough those "unscientific" ecclesiastics were misled precisely because they had accepted science uncritically, since they embraced the Ptolemaic view as final. That the Bible stands as the permanent criterion over against all interpretations of it, is a lesson which churchmen have had to learn. Biblical revelation does not pretend to answer all questions; it commands the subduction of nature, but it does not make science unnecessary; it records the revealed will of God, but it does not render theological effort superfluous. The existence of an absolute is compatible with the existence of an area of relative and provisional knowledge, as well as with the non-existence of it, and a sound statement of Christianity will not minimize the legitimacy of a large area of such experience. By its espousal in certain periods of its history, and by certain of its exponents, of false theology and false science in the name of special revelation, the Christian church has reduced confidence in its claim to possess a final revelation; the identification of such a revelation with temporary viewpoints has encouraged the modern conviction that all knowledge, theological truth included, is probationary. Science, it has been urged, in view of its frank subscription to tenativity, could sustain the shock of reversal, but the theology of special revelation cannot recover from it.

But it is equally true that science, on its side, has fallen frequently into the opposite mistake of affirming absolute truth, after confessing its experimental limitations. Whether one thinks of the dogmatisms with which some scientists, after affirming the provisional nature of their studies, affirmed the finality of viewpoints such as the nebular hypothesis, the Darwinian theory of the origin of species, the mechanical block-universe espoused by many 19th century physicists, an observer of the modern scene can easily find ample illustration of dogmatism on the part of those who disowned all right to dogmatism. The surrender to the urge to substitute some philosophy of science for science itself is not confined, by any means, to the science of theology.

The fact is that no thinker can devoid himself of an absolute, and the modern scientist, like every other human being, will substitute a man-projected absolute for a revelational absolute if he insists upon rejecting the latter. Ancient philosophy worked itself out, in Plato and Aristotle, in the necessity for absolute knowledge, and modern philosophy, despite its disavowal of certainty,[13] has hardly been thoroughgoing in its adoption of the structure of tentativity and change. The modern scientific age, in its beginnings, rejected under the pressure of the new philosophies an appeal to certainty atttained by revelation, but retained the ideal of certainty to be reached by the mathematical method.[14]

---

13. Walter G. Muelder and Laurence Sears state: "The Greek and medieval belief was that man might find an absolute truth. . . This tradition lasted into the modern scientific era on the assumption that it was still possible to reach a final truth independent of the limitations of experience . . The history of modern philosophy is the record of the difficulties which have arisen as men have progressively discovered that the former Absolute was incompatible with this new method" (*The Development of American Philosophy*, 311).

14. John Herman Randal, Jr., notes: "Scientists were attempting to discover a *kind* of knowledge which their very methods made it impossible for them to arrive at: by modern scientific methods of investigation they were trying to reach an absolute system of truth quite independent of any limitations of the mental powers of the essentially imperfect and biological creature that man seems to be.... Their ideal was still a *system of revelation*, though they had abandoned the *method* of revelation" (*The Making of the Modern Mind*, 267. Cambridge: The Riverside Press, 1926, 1940).

It is true indeed that the past two centuries have witnessed the triumph of empirical tentativity over mathematical certainty in the statements of western science; anything resembling an absolute is disowned today as a pre-scientific idol. But for all that, modern science has not really faced the potentially incoherent universe which is latent in its restricted methodology; it has not, that is, discerned with the clarity of the relativists of Greek antiquity what are the implications of an uncompromised empiricism.[15] Contemporary science has a greater debt to its absolutistic forerunners than it acknowledges and indeed, indulges in the ancestal habits of dogmatic absolutism more profoundly than it readily admits. Few indeed are the contemporaries who carry through an exclusively empirical approach to reality with a readiness to accept change as the last word. A. E. Taylor singled out certain "eminent exponents of the 'new physics' " who apply "the 'principle of indeterminacy' in a way which distinctly implies that they mean by indeterminacy pure freakish haphazardness and are in effect saying that the pattern of events is at bottom *incoherent.*"[16] And the plain fact is that the scientific approach to truth is such that it must always acknowledge that truth is unattainable, for it carries with it at every step the demand for revision. It should be clear enough that within empirical limits, science cannot claim inerrancy. But the question is

15. The clichés current on the continent of Europe furnish an instructive contrast with the Anglo-Saxon maxims in this regard. The Americans speak of truth as exclusively derivable from scientific methodology, the Germans of the delusive or unstable nature of truth; the Americans are concerned about great humanitarian causes, the Germans are disillusioned about them (see the interesting study, "Some Axioms of the Modern Man," prepared by Emil Brunner in *Man's Disorder and God's Design*, II, 81-85. New York: Harper & Brothers, 1949).

16. A. E. Taylor, *Does God Exist?*, 6 (New York: The Macmillan Co., 1947).

whether it ever has any right to claim anything other than a greater or lesser restriction of error. The scientist is driven, by his very methodology, to declare that the conclusion which he now offers is not a genuine conclusion, but must be displaced. The point is not merely that science does not tell the whole truth but rather, that at times science does not tell the truth at all.[17] The really deep issue is whether science is entitled to anything beyond mere "methodological assumption" in the interest of facilitating inquiry, and not at all to truth, or whether an inference which is acknowledged to require revision should nonetheless be designated as truth rather than tested opinion.

But if, in view of the tested nature of scientific hypotheses, and the characteristic demand for their revision in terms of further experiment, it be felt that scientific formulas — despite their subjection to and perhaps even inevitability of change — should be classified not under the category of opinion, firmly grounded, but rather under knowledge,[18]

17. Anthony Standen emphasizes both the impossibility of scientific infallible and the necessity for scientific revision. The empirical method can never issue, he stresses, in a theory beyond the possibility of being proved wrong, even if scientists, frequently forget the wrong, even if scientists frequently forget the "faint shadow of doubt which hangs over all their theories" and sometimes regard their work as "pure concentrated essence of objectivity" (*Science is a Sacred Cow*, 28-29. New York: E. P. Dutton and Company, Inc, 1950). After tracing the remarkable development of modern science from Galileo and Newton to the present day, he reminds us that "the same story can be told with a humiliating reverse... if the climax and pinnacle of science is our knowledge of the atom *now,* then what was known ten years ago must have been decidedly imperfect. . . What was known twenty years ago was even more imperfect, and the science of fifty years ago hardly worth knowing. . .what will become of the science of today, some twenty or thirty years from now? Unless the rate of scientific advance shows a notable slacking off... our best knowledge of today will become decidedly frowsy" (*Ibid.,* 32).

18. This is insisted upon with uncompromised firmness by the naturalists, who dismiss every other kind of knowledge and contend that empirical science gives us the only knowledge that we possess.

the question still remains whether this acquaintance with the space-time universe is the only knowledge that we have, both as to method and content. The clearest example of scientific dogmatism is seen when science proclaims as truth not alone that which can be supported only by an appeal merely to a limited area of observation, however wide the range, but that which can be supported by *none*. This is most clearly seen in the naturalistic dogma, so frequently coupled with the modern emphasis that "only what is proved by the scientific method is true," that any supernatural world is simply an illusion. The plain fact is that it is not the supernaturalist, but the naturalist, who here floats his position in this regard without any evidence whatever. The naturalist admits as truth only that which is derived from the scientific method — and that method, by its very nature, is incompetent to rule upon the existence or nonexistence of the supernatural, since it deals only with natural entities. The naturalist and the supernaturalist proclaim with equal vigor that nature is real; beyond this, the naturalist asserts dogmatically (on the basis of a method that inquires only into the natural) that the supernatural is non-existent. The scientific method, to which the naturalist appeals, furnishes no evidence whatever *against* the reality of the supernatural. The naturalist who declares, on the basis of an appeal to the scientific method, that the supernatural is a mere fiction, might just as well deny, as one commentator puts it, that there are only large fish in the Atlantic because, having examined those which he has caught in a net which screens out all the substantial sizes, he finds no small ones.

The impossibility of special revelation or, indeed, of any divine revelation whatever, can be affirmed only within the dogmatic naturalistic bias against the supernatural. For if God exists, what more logical expectation could exist than that He should manifest Himself? A God wholly unrelated to the universe and to man, who exists somewhere in conceal-ment and has not at all disclosed Himself, does not count for very much and, indeed, issues in a world as practically void of God as the naturalist's universe. It is no surprise that, wherever supernaturalism is proclaimed, the ideas of God and of revelation go hand in hand. The naturalist, indeed, projects a universe vacant of God, but for all his rejection of an absolute, he persists upon absolutizing his biases; he heralds the reign of tentativity and relativity, but at the same time proceeds on the latent absolute that nature is *alone* real, that special revelation is therefore impossible. Such a formula, in the end, is more revelatory of the dogmatism of contemporary naturalism than it is of the structure of the case for ultimate reality. The *a priori* declaration, by an empiricist, of what is and what is not possible within the vast reaches of human experience suggests, after all, a source of knowledge, beyond that of empirical tentativity, to which the naturalist pays unwitting witness.

Christianity takes the offensive against this obsession of the impossibility, or even improbability, of special revela-tion, and rejects the limitation of knowledge to the scien-tific method. Christian theism asserts an ultimate truth not verifiable by sense observation and experiment, an absolute which is indeed verifiable, but the evidence for which men obstinately set aside who deal only with relativities and who engage their energies within a limited approach to reality. From the Christian perspective, the reduction of the human knowledge potential to the sphere of the relative is itself an activity of revolt against God.[19]

2. The *superfluity* of special revelation is urged by those who affirm that human reason is able, without it, to attain absolute truth; such revelation would be a needless duplication.   Here, in contrast to naturalism, the quest for certainty is not set aside, but all knowledge is held to be the product of conventional rationalistic process.   The emphasis falls, therefore, upon man's ability to attain ultimate truth apart from special revelation which would be, in view of the competence of human reason, unnecessary and redundant.

Of the alternatives — no absolute knowledge whatever can be attained, some absolute knowledge can be attained by conventional reason, some absolute knowledge is possible by revelation alone — this stream of thought has upheld the second.

Both ancient and modern idealists, and the eighteenth century deists, shared this confidence in human reason, although contemporary idealism frequently abandons, with naturalism, the claim to anything more than probability.[20] Just as for the naturalists of the previous class the denial of humanly attainable absolutes involved the rejection of special revelation, so for these thinkers the assertion of humanly attainable absolutes involves a similar rejection.   The

---

19. The apostle Paul has treated this effort on the part of the natural man to cast out from his inner self the knowledge of God, but not for a moment does he entertain the notion that the venture is genuinely successful; man as sinner succeeds not in the elimination of God, but rather in a substitution of one of an almost infinite variety of false gods for his Creator (cf. Romans 1:18-32).

20. This is a characteristic feature, for example, of Edgar S. Brightman's statement of personalistic idealism: "No knowledge is absolutely certain; all knowledge is subject to revision. . . Religious knowledge could not claim absolute theoretical certainty" (*A Philosophy of Religion*, 166, 194.   New York: Prentice-Hall, Inc., 1940).

common element in both approaches is their hostility to special divine disclosure.

The strength of the philosophical confidence in an absolute attainable by reason alone has usually been the doctrine of divine immanence. God's effective presence in His creation is vitiated, it is held, on any view which requires special revelation for the possession of absolute knowledge. But the immanence as well as the transcendence of God is insisted upon by revelational theism. For once the immanence of God is denied, as in deistic philosophies, the case for the supernatural is destined soon to crumble; to the modern mind, there is not much to choose between deism and atheism, and from the Biblical perspective, man's treatment of the near and living God as if He were remote and quite out of relations is already a practical atheism. It is not, therefore, divine immanence which is the issue at all, but rather the interpretation of that immanence. Biblical revelation, instead of requiring the denial of God's immanence, insists upon it; it does not espouse the view, which in the end proved fatal to deism, that God is exclusively transcendent — a view which raises all kinds of questions about why we know anything about Him at all, and, even if we do, why it matters very much. Deism, quite understandably, went the route from denial of divine immanence to denial of the divine, for a god who is removed from personal relations with man is unrelated to the witness of the divine within ourselves. The equation of divine immanence with man's epistemological competence as a necessary datum is the issue. "The question has to do not with the fact of the divine immannence," as F. W. Camfield has noted, "but with its nature. It will hardly be contended that. . .the truth of divine immanence is so clear and devoid of complications, that it can

forthwith be laid hold of, and made a category for the interpretation of revelation. . . The question arises, are we to
think of the divine immanence as a principle which forthwith
validates the evolution of thought and experience, or are we
to think of it as constantly bringing this evolution to a point
of criticism and new departure. If the latter, it will be evident that we are in no position to estimate the nature of immanence until we have had a revelation from the transcendent."[21]

The philosophic formulation of divine immanence has
tended to absorb man to God in a pantheizing manner. In
the history of philosophy it has been this merging of man
in God, on the psychic side of his being, which has established the possibility of the knowledge of an absolute, so
that the confidence in the competence of human reason has
been sustained by a false view of the nature of man. The
discontentment over this extreme view of divine immanence
comes not only from the side of Biblical theology, but from
recent movements in philosophy, even if these do not rise
to a sufficiently realistic view of the sinfulness of man.[22]
The assumption, therefore, that the Christian view of special
revelation is to be rejected simply because it runs counter

---

21. F. W. Camfield, *Revelation and the Holy Spirit*, 35-36 (New
York: Charles Scribner's Sons, 1934). Camfield's assumption of an
evolutionary view of human development is not essential to the argument, and it is not dealt with here because it is marginal.

22. It is significant that the personalistic view of man, as formulated
by Edgar S. Brightman and Peter A. Bertocci, which avoids the absolutistic merging of man in God by declaring that selves are not a part
of God, compromises philosophic certainty for probability. While Personalism, by placing selves outside of God, seeks to emphasize man's
moral responsibility, it joins with the idealistic traditions in the long run
by denying this. How so? Because it does not regard man as a sinner
in need of atonement; that is, it exempts him from a responsibility that
Christianity assigns to him.

to the accepted formulation of divine immanence in a given era of philosophy is quite naive, and reflects a deeper *a priori* bias than the logic of such an objection permits.

Christianity's view of man as a creature in the divine image maintains a sounder doctrine of divine immanence, avoiding these excesses. Man's nature as finite creature in sin is not such that, from the side of human initiative, it is possible for him reliably to attain the great metaphysical verities. Christianity attacks the rationalistic notion that, apart from special divine revelation, man develops an absolute truth, for this view arrogantly overlooks the creatureliness and sinfulness of man. The indictment of the philosophic confidence in the attainment of an absolute truth by speculation alone grows out of the revelation of God's transcendence as well as immanence, and out of the revelation of man's sinfulness which involves him, as we shall see, in a condition of volitional rebellion.

While rejecting the competence of philosophy to arrive at absolute truth, Biblical theology does not deny that innate absolute truth, independent of special revelation, survives man's fall into sin. The "light that lighteth every man and the "law written on the heart" evidence the fact that God has not left Himself without a witness. But it is a witness stamped upon man antecedent to philosophical establishment.

This denial of the capacity for absolute truth to non-revelational philosophy does not mean, by any means, that philosophy is an illegitimate endeavor, or that Christianity has nothing to learn from philosophy. As long as the relation of revelation and reason is defined as it was in the great tradition of Augustine and the Reformation, that long revelation will involve for men the necessity of exhibiting a more coherent world and life view than any offered by the non-Biblical philosophies.   Philosophy resting on fallacious assumptions, no less than science operating on false bases, will draw polemical fire from Christian philosophers.   But only those who approach the facts with the profoundly un-philosophical assumption that special revelation must be ruled out in advance can disseminate propaganda to the effect that scholars who appeal to special revelation automat-ically do not take philosophy seriously.   The philosophical societies on both sides of the Atlantic include gifted thinkers who are profoundly convinced that not the non-revelational alternatives, but Biblical theology, affords the most coherent explanation of the total movement of men and things.

The issue at stake is the competence of human reason in man's present state.   Secular philosophy refuses to distin-guish his present state from a past state, except by way of improvement, whereas Christian philosophy distinguishes it by way of declension.   For the first time since the Renais-sance, profound thinkers outside the Biblical tradition are acknowledging, in our times, that man has not improved morally over fifty years ago and, if anything, may have lost ground.[23]   In those very circles dominated by liberal theol-ogy, with its revolt to an optimistic view of man, a more "realistic" philosophy of religion has arisen in recent dec-ades, in which the fall of man is once again asserted, and the Adamic account is accorded at least a symbolic, if not an

---

23. Liberal theology has not yet felt the sting of this historical judg-ment.   No period since the beginning of the Christian era was so used as the past fifty years by liberal churchmen, who dominated the evangeli-cal enterprise at almost every propaganda center, in the interest of their social gospel and in the furtherance of social justice related only periph-erally to the New Testament message of personal redemption.

historical, significance.[24] Evangelical theology points to the sinfulness of man as the decisive factor in his relationship with God; only by the elimination of the fact of man's sin can the stream of philosophy, as it has in post-medieval times, assume the competence of human reason in the area of metaphysics.

It must be acknowledged that the Scholastic theology of the Middle Ages itself, by its alliance with Greek metaphysics, helped to obscure the serious noetic effect of sin and thereby aided the concealment of the principle of special revelation. The classic Greek confidence in the competence of human reason in the metaphysical realm, which Christianity had overthrown, became a cardinal emphasis of the early modern rationalistic philosophies which had been encouraged, by medieval theology, to pursue the case for theism by speculative philosophy alone and without appeal to Biblical theology. The synthesis of Thomas Aquinas, which has become the official theology of Roman Catholicism, calls for certainty to be reached by natural theology on the questions of the existence of God and the existence and immortality of the soul. What Thomas did not discern, in an age which was prone to believe rather than to disbelieve, was that when once the case for theism was pursued apart from the environmental conditioning of Christianity, the emphasis on the competence of human reason in the area of metaphysics would work itself around from a case for theism into a case against theism. The sinfulness of man, in Hebrew-Christian theology, goes hand in hand with the necessity for special divine revelation.[25] It was precisely

24. That the recent views of the fall of man are formulated outside the spirit of Biblical theology is, of course, obvious to evangelical scholarship, but that is not the point at issue here.

25. Even evangelical theologians like Charles Hodge, W. G. T. Shedd, A. H. Strong, while repudiating the Thomistic confidence in human rea-

the ruling out of special revelation, as superfluous in the approach to philosophy, which created the astonishing reversal seen in the contrast of ancient and modern philosophy; in the former, idealism overcame naturalism, in the latter, naturalism overcame idealism. It was no longer possible, once philosophy had been acquainted with the God who reveals Himself in a special way, to maintain the case for the supernatural on any lesser ground; the concealment of special revelation came to mean the concealment of the spiritual world.

But this does not mean, as already suggested, that Christianity has nothing to learn from philosophy. Even from anti-Christian philosophy, like the naturalism of Marx, or Nietzsche, or Dewey, it can get some glimpse of how significant meaning departs from life and history in those narrower sensationalistic views of reality; that is, it can learn by contrast. But that is not all. Just because there is no exhaustively anti-Christian philosophy, so that even Marx and Nietzsche and Dewey in different ways yield testimony to the very God they deny, so, too, Christianity can see in every such view, by its inability to work itself out into a comprehensive nihilism, that struggle with the innate image of God which drives every naturalistic philosopher to something less than a consistent outworking of his position. But Christianity can learn more from philosophy than this. The Bible does not answer all the problems which philosophy raises, properly so, in its quest for a comprehensive world and life

---

son, did not fully escape the influence of medieval theology, and constructed a half-way Thomism in the positive significance which they assigned, in a preparatory way, to natural theology. In the case of Strong, this worked itself out finally in a compromise of his evangelical theology with philosophical idealism, more or less in the Lotze-Bowne tradition, but acceptable neither to thorough evangelicals nor personalists.

view. The history of thought at least exhibits the way in which the answers which keen minds have given, from a supernaturalistic as well as naturalistic perspective, have been able or unable to safeguard themselves from modification and reversal, in view of the challenge of subsequent philosophic movements. Whether reality is mental or something additional, what precisely is the role of the human mind in the knowledge situation, — these and a host of questions which have been central issues in the history of philosophy do not lose their importance, simply because one becomes a Christian; if anything, they gain urgency. The validity of the Christian revelation-claim in no way implies the disparagement of whatever truth falls properly into the area of philosophy. The logical laws of identity and difference, and of non-contradiction, which underlie all knowledge, are hardly to be dismissed by Christian theology simply because Aristotle seems first to have formulated them explicity; they are not, after all, an Aristotelian invention, and any sound religious epistemology will hardly be content to dismiss them on the ground that they are peculiar to Greek idealism.

But Christianity has much to teach philosophy, especially since its course has been so much one of indifference to or antipathy for its affirmation of special divine disclosure. Philosophy which declares in advance without any confidence in special revelation, what must and what must not be, is as unphilosophical as modern science is unscientific when it dogmatizes about first principles. The Christian view will be found to have implications for nearly all, if not all, questions which philosophy raises. But Christianity's main service is the clear emphasis that, in formulating its persistent problems, philosophy has tended to overlook that problem which, in the course of human history, is most persistent of all, the problem of sin. Precisely to this problem, more than to the other problems which secular philosophy tends to place in the forefront, the Biblical revelation addresses itself, for nothing less is at stake than man's eternal destiny. Biblical theology deals with man's sin not as a mere incident in time, but as an event in eternity; it deals with special divine revelation from the standpoint of the holy Lord who is the just retributer of man's moral misdeeds. Precisely for that reason, Biblical theology stands in judgment upon all those views which, when they bring special revelation into focus, dismiss it either as impossible because the God who speaks is not accommodated by a naturalistic view of things, or as superfluous because the God who speaks is not allowed to say anything different from what men say by an idealistic view of things. From the standpoint of what Christianity has to teach philosophy, these views are already philosophies in revolt against the holy God, for they counter the doctrine of the sinfulness of man by the doctrine which denies God's ability to declare him a sinner. They absorb man to God, either ontologically, so there is no distinction of being, or epistemologically, so man's thoughts are not beneath God's thoughts, or ethically, so man's acts are not distinguished from God's acts, or in some other manner they affirm the immanence of God so as to conceal the Biblical emphasis also on divine transcendence, ontological, epistemological, and moral.

Sometimes a measure of divine transcendence is affirmed, but it hardly rises to the requirements of the Biblical doctrine of God. The assertion of a limited divine transcendence makes possible a certain emphasis on revelation which nonetheless works itself out into an antagonism, on the ground of superfluousness, of special Biblical revelation. Revelation involving a divine initiative is insisted upon, while at the same time the idea of a special or once-for-all revelation is repudiated. The whole movement of modern idealistic philosophy has partaken somewhat of this emphasis, in contrast with ancient philosophy, since it could not help but be profoundly influenced, even when unsympathetic, by the Hebrew-Christian stress on divine initiative. On this general approach, divine revelation is necessary for the attainment of absolute knowledge, but this does not involve any necessity whatever for a unique or special revelation; rather, absolute knowledge is universally attainable by private religious experience.

This viewpoint strikes directly, therefore, at any thought of a mediated knowledge of God, and insists rather that spiritual knowledge is direct and immediate. This is the common element in all theories of this class, although theories within the class subdivide over such questions as whether the metaphysical revelation is supra-rationalistic or not, or over which of the competitive religions is to be regarded as most adequate, or over the nature of divine transcendence.[26]

---

26. There are as many competitive formulations of divine transcendence as of immanence, although philosophy has not been as explicit in developing the distinctions. Some recent thinkers have caught up P. T. Forsyth's phrase, "the immanence of the transcendent," in the the interest of a quite inadequate view, in which trans-subjective and transhuman elements are found in our experience, but the question which F. W. Camfield asks is not clearly answered: "What has revelation to say *to* these trans-subjective elements in our knowledge and experience?" (*Revelation and the Holy Spirit*, 35, italics supplied). The idealistic emphasis on the all-inclusive Whole, which includes both error and sin in a manner which cancels out their reality, makes only a quantitative distinction between man's knowledge and any revelational knowledge. John Oman (*The Natural and the Supernatural*) and others are still within this frame when they regard man's normative religious conscious-

Proponents of such views sometimes imply that the Christian emphasis on special historical revelation actually voids the general religious consciousness. This complaint has received no meagre encouragement from Karl Barth's view that the vitiation of the divine image in man leaves no point of contact in man for special revelation, so that the Holy Spirit creates His own epistemology which can never be logically appropriated, but which confronts the reason as a paradox to be grasped only in faith. The insistence upon universal divine revelation is one to which Christianity is not, of course, opposed. But that a religious *a priori* exists in the soul of man, and that this religious conscious is not — contrary to the naturalists — to be nullified and voided as referring to no genuine religious object, is a central Christian insistence. The general revelation of God, not only in the realm of nature but in the very mind and conscience of man, is stressed in every sound theology. The real issue concerns not the denial of the general religious *a priori,* but its relationship to special revelation: whether the latter is precluded by the former, whether the former may properly be regarded as an unambiguous preparation for the latter, or whether the fact of sin may not involve consequences so radical that it is quite impossible to equate the general religious consciousness with the subjective possibility of all special divine revelation.

The really strategic element in this affirmation of a universal revelation is the solid fact that there is no such thing as "unaided" human knowledge, but that a divine initiative of some sort is involved in every act of human

---

ness as an intuitive knowledge of the whole of things, derived in all instances from man's permanent continuity with the divine, without any necessity for a revelation that may properly be designated as special.

cognition. In a sense, all knowledge may be viewed as revelational, since meaning is not imposed upon things by the human knower alone, but rather is made possible because mankind and the universe are the work of a rational Deity, who fashioned an intelligible creation. Human reason is not a source of knowledge to be contrasted with revelation, but is a means of comprehending revelation. Unless one is resigned to a deistic view of the world, a view for which the modern mind shows no more preference than the medieval, the process of human cognition can hardly be separated entirely from the immanence of the transcendent God. Thus God, by His immanence, sustains the human knower, even in his moral and cognitive revolt, and without that divine preservation, ironically enough, man could not even rebel against God, for he would not exist. Augustine, early in the Christian centuries, detected what was implied in this conviction that human reason is not the creator of its own object; neither the external world of sensation nor the internal world of ideas is rooted in subjectivistic factors alone. For Augustine conceived the human soul "as constantly dependent on God, who is no more its Creator than its Upholder and Director; and of its intrinsic ideas as, therefore, continuously impressed on it by God... His ontology of 'innate ideas,' accordingly, is that they are the immediate product in the soul of God and Illuminator, always present with the soul as its sole and indispensable Light, in which alone it perceives truth."[27] Nothing could be clearer than that, on

27. Benjamin B. Warfield, *Studies in Tertullian and Augustine,* 143-144 (New York: Oxford University Press, 1930). Warfield's essay on "Augustine's Doctrine of Knowledge" (which appeared originally in *The Princeton Theological Review,* v. 1907, 353-397) is an able study, in which he carefully distinguishes Augustine's view from those pantheistic and idealistic modes of thought according to which God comes to the knowledge of truth in human minds, or man's knowledge simply

Augustine's approach, revelation is the condition of all knowledge, whether sensible or intelligible. To set aside, therefore, the consciousness of God, is to make impossible any solution of the problem not alone of religious knowledge, but of general knowledge as well.[28]

If it cannot be said, as opponents of special revelation sometimes would make it appear, that Biblical Christianity sets aside the general religious consciousness, neither can it be maintained that it compromises the vitality and directness of religious experience in the interest of a second-hand, or remote control, religion by virtue of its mediatorial principle. This is a variant of the effort to dismiss special revelation as a marginal and superfluous type of religious participation. But this complaint can hardly make out its case, for the actual fact is that, contrasted with the other religions of antiquity, it was Hebrew worship which exemplified an intimacy of fellowship with God, and did so precisely in terms of a unique access to Him; and just so, in the western world, it was not the general religious movements, but specifically revelational Christianity, which fixed upon the life and mind of the populace the possibilities of an intimate personal religion in which all temporal relationships were linked to the divine. The truth is that, as Biblical revelation makes apparent, it is actually those "immediated religions" which involve a second-hand spiritual experience, for they

---

coalesces with the Deity's. The dependence of the creature on God, in the knowledge situation, is conceived by Augustine on theistic, and not on pantheistic nor deistic lines, and based not on philosophical, but rather on Biblical considerations.

28. Warfield made Augustine's position obvious in this matter: "Even had man not been sinful, Augustine would never have allowed that he was in a position of himself, apart from God, to do any good or to attain any truth. That would have seemed to him a crass deism, of which he would have been incapable. Even sinless man would have been to him

remain strangers to the special disclosure of God and to the provision of His redemptive grace.[29]

There can be little doubt, if we recur to Augustine again, that the Christian insistence on a mediated knowledge of God did not involve any epistemological circularity which destroyed the vitality of religious experience; instead, he was convinced that sin in the life of man had short-circuited the immediated knowledge of God to the detriment of the spiritual life. "Undoubtedly," Warfield rightly observed, Augustine "teaches that the soul has an immediate knowledge of God."[30] Man's very perception of the ideas or intelligibles of thought involved at once an intuitive perception of Deity.[31] Man is not passive by any means in the acquisition of knowledge, but all genuine knowledge involves divine revelation. But knowledge is conditioned by man's

---

absolutely dependent on God, the Author of all being, the Light of all knowledge, the Source of all good. We have seen him openly teaching that man as man can see light only in the Light; that all truth is the reflection into the soul of the truth that is in God; in a word, that the condition of all knowledge for dependent creatures is revelation, in the wider sense of that term" (*Ibid.*, 161).

---

29. Contemporary Neo-supernaturalism seeks to emphasize the dynamic nature of Christian experience by locating revelation in the encounter, rather than fixing the content of revelation in the Bible, while professing to recognize the Scriptures as a conditional norm, i. e., as the normative witness to revelation. This type of a "first hand" religious experience actually risks the return to immediate experience, which is no Biblical experience at all. In the thought of the Russian mystic Berdyaev, the existential encounter, contrary to Karl Barth and Emil Brunner, provides the mystical basis of the only real understanding of God available, and this inner intuitive awareness takes precedence over the historical revelation in the Bible (Matthew Spinka, *Nicolas Berdyaev: Captive of Freedom*, 103ff. Philadelphia: Westminster Press, 1950). The answer to Berdyaev, in the interest of genuine Christian experience, must not be formulated in terms of an encounter which loses the objective authority of the written Word, or we are back in Mysticism, for then the Word once more becomes "inner" and not "outer."

30. *Ibid.*, 144.

31. *Ibid.*, 148.

nature, as well as by revelation, and this means not alone his intellect, but also his voluntary nature. Man's knowledge is conditioned by his ethical state, which has a determinating effect upon his mental activity.[32] This effect is especially vitiating with regard to the knowledge of God, which stands at the apex of the various orders of truth and requires the maximum purgation for reliability.   Therefore it is not merely the finite and developing nature of the human soul, but its present sinful condition, which complicated for Augustine the problem of religious knowledge, and it is in connection with this moral and spiritual predicament of man that the redemptive revelation of God, as involving a special and unique divine initiative, can alone be understood.[33] The introduction, therefore, of revelation in the narrower, objective form, as the condition of the knowledge of spiritual realities by man as sinner, comes, quite analogously to the entire account which Augustine has given of man's dependence in all states on the creating and sustaining Deity, in the course of a casting of man anew upon God through the latter's redemptive mercy.   Special revelation lifts the reason of man to the lofty knowledge which the turning aside to sin made impossible.

---

32. *Ibid.*, 150.

33. *Ibid.*, 155-156: "Neither the soul's finiteness, nor its mutability. . . need more than warn us of the limitations of our powers and induce in us a becoming humility and patience.   But the invasion of the soul by sin is a different matter.   Here is a power which acts destructively upon the soul's native powers of apprehending truth, blinds the eyes of the mind, distorts its vision, fills it with illusions, so that it sees awry; and a power which so far from passing away with time and growth, battens by what it feeds on and increases in its baleful influence until it overwhelms the soul with falsehood. No merely incomplete, or as yet uncompleted. knowledge accordingly results: but just no knowledge at all, or even anti-knowledge, positive error, vanity, and lies; and thus a condition is created which assuredly calls not for humility and patience, but for despair."

3. The objection to special revelation finds a different turn in the claim that it involves a divine particularism which is immoral. This rejection of the Christian revelation-claim comes not alone from naturalists who discount all supernaturalism, but from supernaturalists who, while not rendering special revelation superfluous by insisting on the competence of human reason to attain absolute truth, nevertheless contend that an historical disclosure, to a particular people at a particular point in space-time, in contrast with a general revelation, involves God in unfairness and partiality. Historical, once-for-all revelation is thus dismissed as a reflection on the love and justice of God. Special revelation is held to reflect a favoritism and party spirit unworthy of a just and loving Deity; any such divine disclosure is precluded as scandalously inequitable.

The objections voiced against special revelation by Douglas Clyde Macintosh may here be taken as rather representative. Appeal to once-for-all revelation is declared to be an "obvious contradiction of the Christian faith in the impartiality and reasonableness of God" for it depicts a God who "purely of his own arbitrary will, works miracles of revelation and faith for some and not for others."[34] Like many recent writers, Macintosh, having reached the limits of an empirical approach which he had set up as the ideal of theological science, postulated as an article of reasonable belief the transcendence of the immanent God. Then it was suggested that God would be guilty of sin, i. e., of injustice and lovelessness, if a special revelation were provided. The assumption made is that God's moral transcendence does not relate man to Himself as a sinner who obscures the effective-

34. D. C. Macintosh, *The Problem of Religious Knowledge*, 342 (New York: Harper and Bros., 1940).

ness of the general revelation, and that if it did, for God to disclose Himself in a special way would be not a merciful but necessarily an unmerciful act.

The most obvious reply to this sort of argument is that, as a matter of historical fact, the world has come to its deep convictions concerning the justice and love of God in the very course of the once-for-all Biblical revelation. The special disclosure of God is not a barrier to, but the very ground, of our confidence in His justice and love. If anything, the modern determiners of what is meant by a just and loving God are those who misunderstand the nature of those divine attributes; they do not know that the problems of justice and justification cannot be divorced, for the God who reveals Himself is the God who makes known His grace and mercy in the provision of redemption. That is the central message of the love of God, by which historic Christianity came first to oppose the loveless gods of pagan philosophy,[35] so frequently resuscitated by modern thought. It might also be noted, as Gordon H. Clark has suggested in a

---

35. Anders Nygren has helped to clarify the "two separate spiritual worlds" which contribute to the making of the Christian idea of love, the New Testament message of Agape and the Hellenistic idea of Eros (*Agape and Eros*, II, 19. London: Society for Promoting Christian Knowledge, 1939). "Agape is primarily God's love, unveiled at its deepest in the Cross of Christ, in His offering of Himself for sinners" (II, 20). How far Macintosh fails to penetrate the true concept of the love of God is apparent, by contrast, from his assertion that "the essentially Christian type of religion and theology is logically defensible, apart from any dependence upon the outcome of historical investigation of the historicity of the Jesus of Christian tradition" (*Op. cit.*, 365). Nygren, on the other hand, has grasped the essential distinctness of the Biblical emphasis on the election love of God, which is far from the Hellenistic starting-point. "One who knows Hellenistic piety," Nygren wrote, "cannot doubt that it is dominated by the Eros motif and has, in principle, no room for the Agape motif. No less clearly, primitive Christianity is dominated by the Agape motif, and Eros is alien to it" (II, 21).

comment to the writer, that love is essentially arbitrary; if it were impartial, it would not be love. A rather impressive case can thus be made for the notion that a god who loves nobody in particular is a loveless god.

This objection to special revelation is seen to derive like the others from an erroneous view of divine transcendence, especially in this case at the moral level. It is not that the Christian emphasis on divine transcendence, whether the divine being, or knowledge, or goodness is meant, cancels out the immanence of God, as the opponents of once-for-all disclosure frequently make it out. That is not the case at all. Christianity emphasizes the fundamental kinship of God and man, but it emphasizes also man's creaturehood, finiteness and sinfulness. And, for Biblical theology, it is not the metaphysical nor even the epistemological barrier between God and man in his created state which erects any special problem, for that is the way in which man was fashioned in the divine image. But it is the moral barrier, set up by the sinfulness of man in his revolt against the holy Lord, which is the great tragedy to which special revelation addresses itself; the fact of sin has had tragic consequences for man in his total relationship with God at every level. The Hebrew-Christian revelation stresses with special primacy this moral transcendence of God. The great gulf that separates man as sinner from the Holy One is overcome alone by the divine disclosure and provision of redemption; there is no path of moral and spiritual union between man and God except through the reconciling work of the Mediator.

That the provision of once-for-all revelation should create the impression of a scandal, should strike man as offensive and libelous, is anticipated by the revelation itself. For the confrontation of man as sinner by the Holy Lord leaves only these alternatives: self-humiliation as sinner, or the denial of his sinfulness by the denial of the revelation which offers a special redemption for sinners who cannot save themselves. The issue is either the acceptance of divinely proffered grace, or a rejection of it as disgraceful. The Bible emphasizes that it is precisely the mind of the sinner in revolt against the holy God to whom special revelation and mediation appear as a scandal, whereas the redeemed sinner knows it as God's call to repentance and salvation.[36] The alternatives are either the disgrace of the sinner, or grace must be disgraced. And, consequently, from the Biblical view of things, that very antagonism for special revelation sometimes said to derive from a delicate moral sense, issues instead from a remarkably defective sense of sin. It derives from spiritual pride, from man's refusal to face the facts squarely with regard to his moral predicament in the sight of the God of holy love, as God Himself makes it known in the special disclosure of the plight of mankind, in view of His offer of rescue.

4. A somewhat different turn is take against special revelation by Floyd H. Ross, professor of world religions at University of Southern California, who contends that it involves a bigotry which looms large as an obstacle to world community. Dr. Ross's antipathy to any particularistic revelation-claim as sheer dogmatism proceeds in his case, as is

---

36. Cf. especially Paul's reminder to the Corinthians concerning "Christ crucified, unto the Jews a stumblingblock, and unto the Greeks foolishness; but unto them which are called, both Jews and Greeks, Christ the power of God, and the wisdom of God" (I Cor. 1:23-24).

apparent from the whole tenor of his volume,[37] from an equally dogmatic antiparticularism, for which the sanction of an unbiased empiricism is illegitimately claimed. But since the impossibiilty of special revelation has been treated already, it is a second feature of the author's thought which here comes into view. That feature is Dr. Ross's insistence that the advocacy of special revelation constitutes an obstacle to world community because it permits no more than "a bow in the direction of respect for personality" and leads to the "logical coercive conclusion" of expulsion from the fellowship.[38] Religious orthodoxy is thus held inevitably to imply intolerance and disrespect for personality, whereas a syncretistic approach alone holds promise, it is asserted, of solution of the problem of world community. But, it may be replied, Dr. Ross nowhere establishes the presupposition so fundamental to his argument, that respect for personality requires the concession that another's theological views are true; fortunately, tolerance has nothing to do with granting the truth of another's theological convictions on this issue, else Dr. Ross would be as guilty of intolerance and disrespect for the personalities of theological conservatives as they would be for the personalities of theological liberals.

The fact of the matter is that Christianity alone, and not syncretism, has the power to realize in any significant de-

---

37. Floyd H. Ross, *Addressed to Christians*: *Isolationism vs. World Community* (New York: Harper and Brothers, 1951). Throughout the volume there occurs not the slightest hint that the living God mighty possibly reveal Himself once-for-all in a normative manner; the very possibility is *a priori* excluded in the most dogmatic fashion. Whereas Ross rejects Christian presuppostions simply because they are absolutistic, he nowhere reckons with the fact that presuppositions in the structure of his own thought are equally absolutistic: e. g., that all theological knowledge is relative, and that the theologian's task is exploratory only.
38. *Op. cit.,* 118, 101.

gree the necessary features of a vital community. The solution of that problem has not come in the past, any more than in the present, by inclusivistic views; every syncretistic approach succeeds only in bleeding a movement of its missionary dynamic. The early church, rescued from Greek and Roman syncretism, found in the supernatural Christ a new love and dynamic which lifted the world from paganism. And Biblical particularism hardly stood in the way of an enlarging fellowship, for Christianity excluded only those who excluded themselves. Christianity alone knew the dynamic for making every man one's neighbor: the unmerited love of the holy Lord for undeserving sinners, exhibited in the substitutionary death of Christ. Sinners who came to Christ knew therefore a love which reaches out to the unworthy, to those to whom there seemed no antecedent indebtedness, and love for whom is not motivated by personal advantage. The Christian fellowship's great commission was anchored in such a love. From the standpoint of the New Testament, Dr. Ross has approached the world problem from the wrong side, for he fails to see that it is man's community with God which needs first to be restored, before a rectification of the social dilemma can follow. And the restoration of this prior community turns, of course, upon God's special revelation and redemption. So that, not theological particularism, but the antipathy to special revelation, turns out to be the real obstacle to a solution of sociological disunity. And disrespect for personality, if we may recur to that aspect of Dr. Ross's objection to Biblical Christianity, belongs more properly to a view which arbitrarily rejects the relevance of divine grace for sinful humanity, than to the Biblical invitation to the restoration of the divine image and the conformity of broken lives to Christ.

5. The case for divine special revelation is grounded in nothing less than the uniqueness of God's dealings with humanity. The distinctiveness of the Hebrew-Christian movement is its declaration of the actuality of once-for-all divine disclosure, justified not in terms of religious postulation, nor simply as a philosophical first principle, but in view of the activity of the self-revealing God. The freedom of God, over against His creation, and His voluntary purpose to redeem man in sin, accounts for the necessity of dealing with special revelation, against all views which dismiss the claim forthwith on the supposed ground of its impossibility, dispensability, unworthiness, or bigotry. Any such *a priori* refusal to examine the merits of the Christian revelation-claim, from the standpoint of Christian theology, not only violates the canons of sound scholarship, but manifests that very speculative arbitrariness which thinkers overgenerously tend to attribute mainly to advocates of competitive views.

By affirming the necessity of special revelation for a satisfactory or "saving" knowledge of God, Christian theology does not imply that an absolute necessity exists for the provision of redemptive revelation within the nature of God. Such a view would destroy the nature of free and gracious redemption. The special disclosure of God's grace came not as an inner obligation or unavoidable necessity, but rather was the display of an unmerited favor. The failure of the Scriptures to suggest that divine redemption is provided for those wicked angels who lapsed from their first estate supplies a caution against any theology which would derive the redemptive revelation from the divine nature by a sort of automatic pantheistic inescapability, as if it involved no divine decision. The Biblical revelation comes in the course of a divine selection and choice, not as the fulfillment of some human expectation of salvation. That God manifests His love to sinful man "without a cause," from the side of human merit, finds frequent emphasis in the Bible. God as the provider of salvation for lost man becomes known only after His special disclosure of the true nature of His love, but prior to that revelation it is a secret.[39]

On the other hand, the divine redemptive disclosure does not appear in Christian theology as a mere appendage to the doctrine of God, as though the nature of the supreme Being could be adequately reconstructed apart from central reference to His provision of salvation for fallen man. The special redemptive revelation of God discloses something essential about the being of God; indeed, it discloses what is most essential about the divine nature, when viewed from the perspective of man's predicament in sin. God is Love, even as He is the Holy One, and the coming of Jesus Christ into history — His life and death — define most clearly the nature of His holy love. At the root of the Biblical distinction between true and false religions stands this emphatic conviction: the non-Biblical religions of works, since they do not take sin seriously and do not teach that God alone can

---

39. Although the reasons for expecting a special revelation may not be satisfactorily maintained, when projected from the side of a man who is no longer a creature in proper relationship with Deity, nonetheless the longing for such revelation is a fact of human history. Even Plato had philosophized that "a man should persevere until he has attained one of two things: either he should discover or learn the truth about them; or if this is impossible, I would have him take the best and most irrefragable of human notions, and let this be the raft upon which he sails through life — not without risk, as I admit, if he cannot find some word of God which will more surely and safely carry him" (*Phaedo*, 85). It was Christianity which gave complete satisfaction to the vaguely felt needs which remained within the prevailing religions and philosophies of antiquity.

and does provide a sufficient salvation for fallen man, are false.

They are false, not because special revelation has no point of contact with general revelation, but because the sinner twists general revelation into an occasion of projecting God in the role of every variety of religious conglomerate. All that has been said earlier, about the reality of general revela-tion, about the presence of some element of truth in every metaphysics, about the immanence of God and the impossi-bility of the reduction of man to sheer animality, does not set aside the stubborn fact that man's state of active spiritual revolt involves him in the vitiation of the knowledge of God and a falsification of his true relationship to the Deity.

It is often protested, against this view, that this denial of competence to human reason involves an utter skepticism, for if man stands in such relations to the world of spiritual truth that he is prone to espouse error, how could he, in any case, come to know and embrace the true God? Just as the emphasis on partial competence of human reason has led from philosophies such as Thomism to the further insistence of modern philosophy on the total competence of human reason, so, it is suggested, the case for the incompetence of human reason in the realm of metaphysics is said to involve, in its logical outworking, the impossibility of any genuine knowledge of God. And so indeed the relativistic philoso-phy of the ancient Sophists, with its stress on the intrinsic tension of the knowledge situation, worked itself out into agnosticism. But by the incompetence of human reason Christianity intends something quite different from any such notion as, that the forms of thought do not extend to the divine, or that God is not a proper object of human concep-tion. Christianity asserts, in fact, the very opposite; it points back to a genuine knowledge of God and, what is no less important, points out to wayward man the means of overcoming his present predicament. That man's spiritual separation from the Creator and Lord of his being can be surmounted, and that failure to overcome it involves an element of human decision and negation, is a central feature of the Biblical view of the Divine-human relationship. Special revelation and redemption, rather than constituting an obstacle to the overcoming of this barrier, are the precise means of its elimination. The supernatural regeneration of sinners secures the acceptance of the divine revelation as true, on the part of individuals who previously disputed its truth. If the incompetence of human reason, in the Bible meaning of that phrase, issues in skepticism in religious matters, it does not do so by any intrinsic necessity of the Biblical estimate of man. Rather, the rejection of special divine revelation as leading to skepticism only furnishes a further evidence of the depth of man's revolt against God: divine disclosure is absorbed to incredulity, divine redemption to mythology, and the sinfulness of man to a radical reflection on his moral achievements.

The rejection of God's specially revealed Word, as well as all disobedience to the holy Lord, is referred by the Scriptures to "pride," as the root of sin. In this emphasis on man's pride, and on its desirable opposite, humility, the Hebrew-Christian revelation stands apart from the other world religions and moral systems. The emphasis falls on man as a rebel, attributing to himself the honor and glory that are God's. Actually, his walk before God is a radical contrast with the lowliness of Christ in the incarnation, which wrote the virtue of humility into the pattern of a devout life. For man in sin seeks an independent solution of his problems; he will not turn to God, for that would involve the acknowledgment of his moral bankruptcy, of his need to be "saved." That is why the Bible speaks of the "wisdom of God" appearing to be "folly" to "those who are perishing" (I Cor. 1:18). There is no humiliation for the proud mind and heart more radical than confessing that the mind is at the end of its tether, that the will has been directed toward evil ends, that the emotions have been fixed upon perverse idols — that one is lost and cannot save himself, but throws himself upon the forgiving mercy of God for salvation. Hence it is a "more comfortable" road for the sinner to extend scientific tentativity to the whole area of truth (for this undermines the finality of the Christian revelation-claim) or to admit absolutes only of human discovery (for this links man to the eternal by a direct continuity so as to conceal his sinfulness). Either of these alternatives conceals his utter dependence upon God; that is why they are such favorite options in an era of special revolt against Him.

Not any lack of evidence for special revelation, not any necessity for crucifying reason, not any violence done to a coherent view of things, but the assertion of human autonomy, and independence, over against the sovereign Lord, is at the basis of the revolt against the Christian revelation-claim. For that claim is not alone a gnosis about the supernatural; it is at once an altar call, a summons to repentance and salvation. It is not because of a facing of the facts, but because of a refusal to come to terms with them, that men reject this summons. The spurning of God's justification of the sinner, by His grace in Christ Jesus, mean that men think they can justify themselves; the rejection of His authority means their preference for human authority; the refusal to hear His Word means the autonomy of human reason. In the end, the rejection of the special revelation means the enthronement of the sinner and the discard of Hebrew-Christian values, for they cannot be separated from the redemption that is in Christ Jesus.

If now we are concerned with the once-for-all, historical Biblical revelation which Reformation Christianity and evangelical theology affirm, it must be distinguished promptly from pseudo-varieties of the Christian revelation-claim which have come to the fore in our own time. Such sub-Biblical views have issued from scholars who, revolting against some of the central features of liberal philosophy of religion, nonetheless have been unable to divorce themselves from other modern and critical biases which require a compromise of Biblical theology. Consequently they vigorously affirm a theology centered in the God who reveals Himself in a special way, but the special way turns out to be disturbingly less than a satisfactory Biblical view, and thus after all a competitive formula. This must be said of neo-supernaturalistic scholars like Karl Barth and Emil Brunner in their call for a reassertion of the centrality of once-for-all, historical, Biblical revelation. For their representation of "once-for-all," "historical," "Biblical," "revelation" comes to mean something quite different from what evangelical theology has understood by these terms.

Neo-supernaturalism's once-for-allness marks a departure from Christian theology because it replaces the God who has spoken by the speaking God. In two ways this compromises the orthodox view of special revelation; one, in that the Bible no longer transmits revelation to us, according to the newer theology, and again, in that we ourselves must contribute to the event of revelation presumed to exist in our age as well as in the Old and New Testament eras. Contrary to the New Testament emphasis on "the faith once for all delivered to the saints,"[40] this view conceives revelation not as divine truth imparted once-for-all, so as to require its transmission by prophets and apostles. Rather, the once-for-allness is applied to the invariable content which remains changeless while the experience of revelation is repeated, today as in the past; the impartation of revelation is not limited to prophets and apostles, but is made to us as well. Revelation does not, for Barth, take place except in terms of personal response; consequently, the personal response of the believer involves him in the consummation of divine revelation.[41]

Nor, when Neo-Supernaturalism speaks of historical revelation, does it mean what Christian theology has intended by that term. For only ambiguously does it relate revelation to history; revelation itself occurs only in super-history, which is intended to designate not miracle-history accessible to the general historian, but rather the existential

---

40. There can be little doubt that the Word *hapax*, here (Jude 3) used for once-for-all, is contrasted with the notion of what is repeatable, in the interest of what has happened at a specific point in time and space; cf. its use in I Pet. 3:18 and Heb. 9, 26, 28, of Christ's suffering for sin; in Heb. 9:27 of human death; and also in other connections in II Cor. 11:25, I Th. 2:18, Phil. 4:16, and Heb. 9:7, 10:2, 12:26. What is precisely excluded by Jude 3 is the notion of the repeated delivery of the content of the Christian faith.

41. It is not surprising, therefore, that H. R. Mackintosh should have asked "how the 'once-for-allness' of the event of revelation in Jesus Christ is to be harmonized with the contention that revelation, as complete, includes man's believing acknowledgment of its reality. Is the 'givenness' of revelation in Christ quite real and unconditioned, if after all, to be fully realized, it must be apprehended. . . Is not God's gift of Himself in Christ fully real whether it be received or not?" (*Types of Modern Theology*, 281. London: Nisbet and Co. Ltd., 1945).

encounter.[42] It is never made clear why, if the entire Adam-relationship of man as sinner can be flouted in terms of myth, i. e., of a symbolic rather than a historical fall, the Christ-relationship of man as redeemed cannot be divorced from any actual historical incarnation. The tendency of both Barth and Brunner to treat the incarnate Christ as a "pointer" or "witness" to revelation, rather than as the high point of the divine manifestation to man, as indeed the New Testament seems everywhere to presuppose, indicates that, in their definition of revelation, the historical element is more marginal and less central than Christian theology has maintained. The words of Herbert Butterfield, the Cambridge historian, are well chosen: "It would be a dangerous error to imagine that the characteristics of an historical religion would be maintained if the Christ of the theologians were divorced from the Jesus of history."[43] Such a divorce, of course, is disclaimed by neo-supernaturalistic theologians. But their emphasis falls upon the witness of the Holy Spirit in such a way as to move the historical content of Christian revelation to the margin, in a way that hardly satisfies the requisites of a stable evangelical theology.

It should be clear from this that there is ground for suspicion that the neo-supernaturalistic view of revelation is not to be identified as Biblical in the orthodox sense. The fact is that theologians like Barth and Brunner refuse to

42. This comes to view especially in Brunner's insistence that belief in the resurrection of Christ is a consequence of belief in Christ, and not vice versa. There is no denying that belief in Christ's resurrection is accompanied by the context of his life and claims and works, so that the event itself may be seen as congruous with His person; it would be folly to rest the deity of Christ on the undisputed bodily resurrection of a person of whom men know nothing else. But that the bodily resurrection of Christ is no way contributes to our ground of faith in Him in the disputed assumption in Brunner's view.

43. Herbert Butterfield, *Christianity and History*, 129. London: G. Bell and Sons Ltd., 1950.

identify the content of revelation with the Bible. They reject, that is, the Reformation view that revelation is inscripturated, that the Scriptures are the divine provision of the Word of God written. The Bible is viewed as an indispensable witness to revelation, which is confined to the existential encounter; it is not, however, an infallible norm, for it contains errors of a scientific and historical nature, and possibly even of a theological and ethical nature.[44] The content of revelation is thus not anything that is written in the Bible; the content of revelation is communicated only in the divine-human encounter. The Bible, and church proclamation, are witnesses to the reality of revelation in the encounter. It is clear from this that Neo-Supernaturalism, by its assertion of Biblical revelation, does not mean what orthodox theology has understood by that term, that the will of God for man is inscripturated.

If the "once-for-allness," the "historicalness" and the "Scripturalness" of the neo-supernaturalistic view of divine disclosure has been called into question, even more serious objection has been taken to its central concept of revelation itself. For revelation is here defined not in propositional terms, but rather, in terms of paradox. Revelation is asserted to be intrinsically paradoxical and non-conceptual, so that it necessarily confronts the recipient as incoherent, and must be appropriated only by faith, and not on logical grounds. Such a view would eliminate any appeal to coherence as a test of truth and would give no reason for responding to some paradoxes and not to all. The appeal to the witness of the Spirit here is of no aid, for either the Spirit's witness is ranged on the side of coherence or it is not; if so, the emphasis on intrinsic paradox must be

44. Cf. Barth, *Dogmatik*, I, 2, 565.

waived.[45] In the history of theological thought, the proper terminus of such a view, which denies the overlapping of human ideas with the religious object, is unbelief rather than faith in God; the neo-Kantian movement to skeptical illusionism and agnosticism, represented by Ludwig Feuerbach, A. Lange, and Hans Vaihinger, rather than the neo-supernaturalistic alternative, is the final outcome of any such radical repudiation of coherence in the interest of antinomy and paradox in the realm of religious knowledge. The Tertullian formula, that Christianity involves belief in the absurd, and hence the crucifixion of reason, has not been at any time the prevailing or accepted formulation of the relationship between reason and faith.[46] The most acceptable statement of that relationship finds in faith a means to understanding, so that the special disclosure of God provides human thought with an adequate coherence, removing the tensions and contradictions of philosophies formed within the limited and distorted insights of mankind in sin, and furnishing at last a satisfying rationale of things. Special revelation, instead of being destructive of rationality and coherence, is properly seen to be the guarantee thereof. Human reason and special revelation have their ultimate ground in the same unique source, the holy Lord of the universe.

---

45. In a note to the writer, Gordon H. Clark points out that paradoxes and propositions cannot be contrasted; a paradox exists when two propositional statements cannot be reconciled. A curious commentary is furnished by Brunner on his own position when, in *The Christian Doctrine of God*, where he rejects the doctrine of predestination in the following way: "A non-reflective faith. . .can tolerate the paradox: being predetermined and being responsible. But when men began to *think*, this primitive formulation was not sufficient" (*Ibid.*, 317. Philadelphia: The Westminster Press, 1950).

46. Cf. the chapter on "The Reasonableness of Christianity" in the writer's *Remaking the Modern Mind*, 219-239 (Grand Rapids: Wm. B. Eerdmans Publishing Company, 1948, 2nd ed.).

THE RECENT THEOLOGICAL
PERPLEXITY

IV

The Recent Theological Perplexity

FIFTY years ago Protestant Modernism in its classic expression was already, in many places, fifty years old and more; everywhere it seemed to be arriving at a vigorous maturity which enabled it to capture, one after another, the propaganda centers of the evangelical enterprise. There was little outward evidence that Modernism was suffering from a congenital sickness so that, in another fifty years, it would be acknowledged, even by some of its former champions now aligned both on theological right and left, as a dead viewpoint, and that some scholars would insist it survived only where there was an ideological culture lag or where professors and pastors were ready to die for the old party line at whatever cost.

Walter Marshall Horton has singled out the period 1850-1914 as "the great age of liberalism." The latter date was not intended to indicate that the first World War ended the strenuous struggle which Modernism waged against evangelical Protestantism; surely the career of that Baptist champion of Fundamentalism, W. B. Riley, testified that classic Liberalism, even in the years of its decline, had accumulated to itself a powerful ecclesiastical machine strong enough to bend many a theological effort into conformity. But the first World War wrote into history in bold letters what the subsequent course of events has served only to italicize, that the optimistic assimilation of man and history to God, which stood at the center of the classic Liberal outlook, stood discredited by realistic interpretations of the sociological drift of our era. Even within the so-called empirical approach, which Fundamentalism insisted with one eye on Biblical theology was never "empirical enough," it became increasingly difficult for Liberal theology to demonstrate man's direct moral continuity with the divine. Nothing is clearer than that, since the first World War, classic Modernism has fought a series of delaying actions which, by 1950, had been unable to offset the conviction that its theological system is an undesirable formulation which at all events must be superseded. The theology of Modernism, remarkably enough, had been unmasked as profoundly unscientific.

As one surveys the past half century of theological activity, he is struck by such a diversity of tendencies as to proclaim almost at once that it is obviously an era of theological fragmentation, lacking a sense of unity even at the deepest levels. In such an era of intellectual turmoil, leading theologians themselves will reflect profound disagreement over the most significant trends, simply because they interpret the movings of thought from rival perspectives.

Thus, for one thinker, the striking theological peculiarity of the period is that it marked the "rediscovery" of divine immanence in a sense in which Reformation theology had obscured it; for another, that it witnesses the "recovery" of that Reformation emphasis on divine transcendence which Modernism had concealed. Such centers of interest, from whatever theological bias the period is viewed, press readily to the fore. There is the seeping into the American scene of Buddhist thought under the guise of Christian no less than philosophic terminology; there is Walter Rauschen-

busch's first book, *Christianity and the Social Crisis* (1907),
coming as a forerunner of the social gospel; there is the
fundamentalist-modernistic controversy of the early twenties,
which is recalled in one circle in terms of "stalwarts of Biblical Christianity like John Roach Stratton, J. Gresham Machen, I. M. Haldemann, Curtis Lee Laws, and W. B. Riley,"
and in another circle in terms of Stewart Cole's evaluation
of Fundamentalism; there is the rise of the clinical training
program for theological students which, in humanistic circles, enables the clergyman who has sacrified an objective
Word of God to become a professional social case worker;
there is the loosening of the grip of scientific, reductionistic
Naturalism on the thought of many leaders; there is the
dissatisfaction with the old-line Liberalism and the mount-
ing revolt, recalling Reinhold Niebuhr's *Moral Man and
Immoral Society* (1932) and Harry Emerson Fosdick's
article, "Beyond Modernism," in the *Christian Century*
(Dec., 1935); there is the decreasing confidence in human
self-sufficiency and a new disposition to reconsider the doctrine of original sin; there is the new concern with the
evangelical and personal over against the liberal concern
primarily with the history of religion and social gospel problems; there is the turning away in many quarters from the
primacy of philosophical to Biblical theology, in terms of a
"new biblicism" which is frankly critical but emphasizes the
concept of revelation; there is the "deeper" sense of the
corporate character of the church.[1]

On another occasion an opportunity was provided your
lecturer to pass in review, from the standpoint of the mov-

---

1. Each of these was singled out as a significant trend in the theology
of the past fifty years in America by a group of representatives theologians to whom an inquiry was addressed.

ing history of the half century just closed, the striking events and ideas around which the fortunes of Protestant theology have revolved in our times.[2] What may be more useful, on this occasion, is a survey of the varied meanings which the competitive philosophies of religion have imported, in our generation, into the theological vocabulary hallowed by the Christian revelation. By the contemporary drift of ideas this sacred vocabulary — including not alone key Biblical words like "revelation," "rebirth," but indeed the whole gamut of terminology from "God" to "man" — has been less honored than secularized. And even the secularizations have not followed a single mold, as we shall see. Modernism and Humanism reduced the vocabulary of supernaturalism into competitive notions. Almost a century ago, Henry Mansel observed, in delivering a lecture in a famous series across the seas, how the vague generalities of the philosophy of religion frequently gain a vigor and vitality by their identification with sacred concepts. "A religious association," he remarked quite appropriately, "may sometimes serve to disguise the real character of a line of thought which, without that association, would have little power to mislead. Speculations which end in unbelief are often commenced in a believing spirit. . . An unstable disciple often tears off strip by strip the wedding garment of his faith, — scarce conscious how the language of Christian belief may remain almost untouched, when the substance and the life have departed from it."[3] In our day, the lack of alertness that the substance has departed is more frequently to be found

---

2. Cf. the writer's *Fifty Years of Protestant Theology* (Boston: W. A. Wilde Co., 1951) for a survey of the recent tensions in their historical unfolding.

3. Henry Mansel, *The Limits of Religious Thought* (Bampton Lectures 1868), 70f. (London: John Murray, 1870).

among genuine believers, who are not aware of the extent to which concepts which are cherished by them are employed in a competitive sense by contemporary minds.

Thus it may be helpful to scour some of the central concepts of theology and, by way of theological dictionary, to contrast in concise fashion the content which some of the vigorous schools of thought on the contemporary scene intend by the use of terms familiar to us all.

This theological subtraction and reduction represents only half the confusion of the current religious scene. For it is not only the naturalistic distortions of Biblical terminology with which evangelical Protestantism must now contend. Supernaturalistic movements today making an appeal, frequently in the very name of historic Christianity, are also found to be importing a sub-Biblical content into theological concepts which are hallowed by the Gospel tradition. Not only Roman Catholicism, in its contemporary Neo-Scholastic expressions, but also Neo-Supernaturalism, that higher Liberalism which has in our generation come to the fore as a chastened successor to the Modernism of a generation ago, must be referred to in this regard. The Biblical terminology is thus sometimes as frequently exploited in the house of its professed friends as in the camp of its admitted enemies.

The concepts of God, revelation, man, Jesus Christ, redemption, are familiar to us all; what may not be equally familiar is the varying content which is assigned to these central theological concepts by contemporary movements, such as evangelical Protestantism, Roman Catholicism, Neo-Supernaturalism, Modernism, and Humanism. These movements may be singled out for effective contrast, since they furnish rather representative points of differentiation in their theological alignments.

To evangelical Protestantism, the obscuring of special Biblical revelation will always appear as one of the major theological characteristics of our era. Revelation, in this sense, finds its meaning for an evangelical in the truths about God and His relations to His creation which have been disclosed by special divine initiative and inscripturated. The Roman Catholic view of revelation, which is as much as ever a competitor on the American theological scene, assigns equal value to the Bible and to church tradition, and concentrates revelation in the supposedly infallible interpretation of the teaching Church, especially the Pope. The more recent Neo-Supernaturalistic view, associated particularly with the names of Karl Barth and Emil Brunner, regards the Bible merely as a "witness" to revelation which presumably occurs continuously in a personal encounter with God conditioned upon human response, and denies the very possibility of doctrinal revelation, combining its affection for special, historical revelation with an evolutionary and higher critical approach to the Scriptures. Modernism, having sacrificed special revelation and miracle to the recent philosophy of science which insisted on the absolute uniformity of nature, absorbed special revelation to general revelation, regarded as simply another way of viewing the process of human insight from its upper side, and yet professed to salute Jesus Christ in His moral demands absolutely. Humanism, with its clear-cut denial of the reality of the supernatural, eliminated the ambiguity of the modernist's appeal to the so-called scientific method and recognized no legitimate function to be designated as revelation in distinction from human insight, subject to revision, gleaned through the application of the scientific method of sense observation and verification; here the concept of revelation, if admitted at all, is thoroughly secularized.

It is no idle observation, often made in the course of theology and philosophy, that the concepts of God and revelation stand or fall together. The varying views of God involve contrasting views of revelation. One of the great emphases of contemporary theology is that the Christian doctrine of God, least of all, ought to be constructed apart from its special emphasis upon its *Erkenntnissweg,* or path of knowledge. For evangelical Protestantism, God is that eternal supernatural Being, three persons in one essence, who is self-revealed as the sovereign moral creator of all things by an act of free volition. The Roman Catholic view of God is formally the same, except that, because of the extent to which Scholastic theology leans upon Aristotelian metaphysics, God's living confrontation of humanity is concealed by philosophical abstractions and speculations. The God of liberal theology has never been uniformly determined; insofar as the personality of God was retained, this was done along unitarian, rather than trinitarian, lines; the divine transcendence, ontologically, morally and epistemologically, was obscured by the acceptance of an extreme view of divine immanence; the grace of God was lost in a sentimental view of divine love. Neo-Supernaturalistic theology views God as triune personal activity, without clearly rising above the concessions of a modalistic view; it insists upon the ontological, moral, and epistemological transcendence of God, developed at times with a non-Biblical radicalism. The humanistic views, when they retained the vocabulary of theism, reacted against Modernism to the philosophical left, rather than to the right as did Neo-Supernaturalism. In these views, the liberal ambiguity over the personality of God is evaporated in conformity with the demands of a naturalistic view; God is simply the moving front of the evolutionary process, and if spoken of as personal, this is intended merely as a symbolic representation of the fact that the universe by its production and continuance of personal creatures exhibits itself — to this point in time — as "friendly," or at least, as not "hostile" to them.

The nature of man is, in every period of thought, a central concern. In this area of definition too the modern mind has been beset by a lack of unanimity which reflects the contemporary cultural confusion. For Biblical theology, exhibited by evangelical Protestantism, man is a distinct species, created by a divine act in a state of primal holiness, from which the first man and representative of the human race Adam fell by voluntary transgression, implicating his posterity in guilt, corruption and penality; hence man is, at the core of his personality, a sinner, whose moral ideals and attainments rest under divine displeasure, so that he is exposed to divine wrath; the divine standard of morality is achieved on his account only by the Redeemer, in justification, and in gratitude for divine grace, man, in the strength of a supernatural dynamic, seeks to realize conformity to the divine will. Roman Catholic theology is essentially a compromise of this Biblical anthropology. It retains the doctrine of a fall from primal holiness, but since man is regarded as having been created in a state of moral innocence or neutrality rather than positive holiness, and conceives the latter as a reward for his continued obedience, the loss of original righteousness does not involve the loss of an essential element of his created state. Therefore, the Roman Catholic doctrine of man, while not optimistic in

that it insists upon the necessity of salvation by divine provision, does not emphasize depravity in such a way as to
stress the epistemological and volitional effects of the
Adamic fall. The sinfulness of man, therefore, is coupled
here with an emphasis that salvation, as we shall see later,
is by both faith and works, and is merged also with an
emphasis that human reason is partially competent in the
area of metaphysics so that natural theology is viewed as
the legitimate avenue to revealed theology. In the case of
other contemporary views, the modern philosophy of evolution has resulted in striking changes in the doctrine of man,
since they assume the evolutionary origin of man.[4]

Modernism abandoned man's primal holiness, and derived
the first man through an advancing animal ancestry, and
limited man's responsibility to those ethical choices which
fall within his present powers of realization, so that, by the
denial that he is in a state of sin and corruption, and consequently of the necessity for divine regeneration, and by
the emphasis upon the divine immanence which carries
forward the evolutionary process at the summit of which
man has appeared, it led on to the optimistic view of the
essential goodness of man. Neo-Supernaturalism, in its
recent revolt against this optimistic doctrine of man's
essential continuity with God in his present state of sin,
combines Biblical revelation and scientific philosophy and
empirical observation in a remarkable synthesis which the
partisans of each of these approaches eye with considerable
curiosity. The essential sinfulness of man and the necessity

---

4. Actually, the Roman Catholic hierarchy has not ruled one way or
the other on the issue of evolution, except to insist upon the divine
origination of man, so that the emphasis on man as a creation in the
divine image is coupled with evolutionary views which sometimes, with
regard to the remainder of creation, are scarcely distinguishable from
naturalistic evolution.

of a divinely provided salvation come again to the fore, but by way of competition with orthodox theology. Neo-Supernaturalists, in their view of man, surrender the primal holiness of the first man to the evolutionary theory and insist upon not a historical but a symbolic or transhistorical fall; the story of the fall of Adam is the story of each of us, who because of anxiety at the juncture of the worlds of nature and spirit translates his ideals into reality by the inclusion of an egoistic provision and thus vitiates a pure altruism. Such a view, as the writer has indicated elsewhere, is at once too optimistic and too pessimistic about human nature to satisfy the requirements of the Biblical theology which it claims to serve.[5] Although this anthropology again proclaims man's "responsible inability," by virtue of its insistence on the inevitability of sin it cancels out the significance of what it reaffirms, and hardly reinstates a Biblical view of man. The humanistic view of man, once again, eliminates the inconstancy of the modernistic appeal to the implications of the naturalistic philosophy of science for man; just as the neo-supernaturalistic trend seeks to orient modernistic anthropology more alertly toward the supernatural, so the humanistic trend has sought to insert man wholly within the context of the world of nature. Here all talk of a supernatural image in man, by virtue of his participation in some way in an unchanging rational and moral realm of spirit, is renounced in accord with the strict requirements of naturalistic formula. Man, essentially an animal, is differentiated from other animals not by any reference to a supernatural realm, for no such sphere

---

5. Cf. the writer's *The Protestant Dilemma*, 134ff., in which the view of Reinhold Niebuhr especially, who speaks for the American realistic theologians more than for the German dialectical theologians, is considered.

is admitted, but rather because he is craftier, being able, by virtue of his production of techniques for mastering his environment, within limits to subdue it to his advantage. Here morality is given not a theological but an anthropological or sociological sanction only; sin is evaporated into a culture lag or into the failure to live by those ideals to which the most "advanced" community has attained, subject always to critical revision; grace is simply the reliability of nature in its processes in the course of man's adjustment to them. Whether this humanistic anthropology gets an optimistic, pessimistic, or cautiously neutral interpretation, depends upon how seriously its advocates take the emphasis of the evolutionary theory on the necessity that all forms of life are to be considered as only moments in the process, destined to be replaced by more advanced forms. Since humanism regards nature, not mind, as of ultimate significance, the presence in man of rational and moral faculties is not regarded as any guarantee of his permanent significance.

If there is another term which, by exhibiting its implications in the contemporary marketplace of theology and philosophy of religion, will hold before us the lack of unanimity in an age which has been in revolt against the Christian faith in its Biblical expression, it is the term "regeneration." Evangelical Protestantism, with its Biblically-alert emphasis on the sinfulness of man and the necessity for a salvation which God provides, has championed the necessity, on the part of the individual, for a repentance and faith upon the condition of which divine forgiveness is available, on the ground of the expiatory death of Jesus Christ for sinners, and which issues, by a supernatural activity of the Holy Spirit, in the subsequent life of the believer, in the birth of a new nature so that the whole man, in his thoughts, emotions and volitions, is disposed Godwards, through continual sanctification. In contrast with this, the theology of Modernism, which by its elimination of miracle and heightened emphasis on divine immanence had pared from Christian belief and life any need for the substitutionary atonement of Christ and for a supernatural regeneration, intended by "rebirth" something remarkably different from evangelical theology. Applying, as it thought, the scientific method to the conversion experience, it determined that the constant factor in all such crises was that the individual in question was delivered from a state of personality tension and discord with its inner insecurity to a state of tranquility and confidence in which a unification of personality resulted by the surrender of one's life, with its lack of a unified moral demand, to following the example of Jesus Christ in his absolute ethical claim. Thus the modernistic missionary message, as against the other religious movements, was that Jesus better than any other religious or moral genius could, in virtue of his ethical code and example, thus unify discordant personalities around His peerless moral example. It was at this point that humanistic philosophy struck hardest against the modernistic perspective. The humanists challenged the modernists, in view of their appeal to an empirical scientific methodology, over their peculiar reverence for the person and message of Jesus. A scientific methology, Humanism affirmed, knows no exceptions from its dictum that all conclusions are subject to further criticism and revision; the ascription of absoluteness to Jesus — even a "relative absoluteness" which expressed a cautious faith, unbuttressed by evidence, that he would never be surpassed — was asserted to be as much a violation of a genuinely scientific spirit as the fundamentalist's confidence in the reality of miracles. Therefore Humanism did not hesitate to apply its presuppositions to the conversion experience. Since the essence of the experience, insofar as it is observable to the recognized techniques of empirical observation and verification, is the deliverance from inner tension and discord to an outlook in which the personality is integrated and unified, whatever achieves such a result for the individual is to be regarded as divine, i. e., as worthy of the total surrender of one's life, whether it be some socially-directed agency, such as the Red Cross, March of Dimes, or other worthwhile social service effort, or some noble ideal, such as world peace or world government, or whether it be some dynamic personality, such as Socrates, or Copernicus, or Jesus. Here the idea of rebirth works itself out on completely secularized lines, and includes as an essential ingredient the dismissal of the supernatural as a prerequisite for the unity of outlook which the humanist seeks. It is curious that the newer existentialistic and neo-supernaturalistic views abandon entirely the idea of deliverance from tension; rather, the crisis experience is made normative, and redemption consists for them essentially, in some expositions of it, in the commitment of life to Christ's law of love in such a way that the objectification and de-personalization of man and God is overcome by an intensified mystical personalism.

Surely it is evident from all of this that nothing characterizes the outlook of the mid-twentieth century more than a lack of agreement on central issues which give life meaning and perspective. Such views as those exhibited in competition above, running the whole gamut of affirmation, positive and negative compromise, and denial, are not the isolated positions of uninfluential thinkers scattered here and there. Instead, they are the views of the centers of cultural influence, exhibited in their diversity and disagreement. And that very discord, manifesting the lack of a spiritual unity at the center of our way of life, is of momentous import. A culture which has lost its unanimity concerning the validity and significance of the spiritual and the moral is not a culture which is doomed to disintegration at some future day; rather, it is culture in the very process of disintegration. Historians looking back upon our times from some distant vantage point will not fix upon some future date as the transition point dividing the stage of cultural cohesion from that of cultural degeneration; that point has already been passed. All that remains for the future, unless there is a moral and spiritual renewal on a scale in which it is not yet in evidence, is for history to eventuate in some great debacle which, just as the sack and fall of Rome was the occasion after which one spoke of Graeco-Roman culture as something obviously in the past, will provide an equally graphic external symbol of the end of an era.

As in a long-distant age, the descendants of Noah sought by a combination of the forces of man to build in the sight of the heavens a tower which would perpetuate their memory, only to find their speech, which is a minimal requisite of common action, under a divine judgment which removed their last remaining bond of unity, so in our times the secularistic infiltration of the vocabulary of the West has robbed men of an understanding of life and themselves, so that the story of Babel seems remarkably contemporary. If that be so, the story of Pentecost too could, once again, take on a remarkably contemporary character also. For there, by the divine miracle of grace, men of many nations and tongues, of many classes and temperaments, found that a multiplicity of languages is no barrier to a unified world, provided they find their central unity in the Word become flesh for the salvation of lost mankind.

THE CHRISTIAN AND LIBERAL
STARTING-POINTS

V

The Christian and Liberal Starting-Points

AMONG many schools of thought today there is formal agreement that America's survival and, in fact, that of free nations everywhere, depends in the long run upon vital spiritual commitment.

This formal agreement is coupled, as we have already indicated, with thorough disagreement over the proper and preferable content of the terms vital, spiritual, commitment. It is not too much to say that, as far as it concerns the western world which was rescued once from paganism by the power of the Christian message, this disagreement is more the product of the religious phenomenon called Liberalism than of any other force. For it was in the name of Liberalism that Biblical supernaturalism was dissolved into philosophy of religion, and Christianity dismissed at its central points of interest as legend and mythology. Roman Catholicism beyond doubt had perverted central emphases of the Biblical message, but nonetheless it had erected in medieval times a culture about which the major element was its relationship to the specially-revealed God. Liberalism dissipated interest in the specially-revealed God, on the authority of the specially enlightened modern man.

The differences which separate the evangelical and liberal interpretations of Christianity are far-reaching, and any effort to minimize them, as if they were secondary or unimportant, can only be the product of confused thinking.

Liberalism can be true to its own genius only while it regards Christianity as an expression of an essence common to all religions, while it views Christian experience as a variety of universal religious experience, while it represents the incarnation as a divine-human relationship which has its parallels in the non-Christian faiths, while it assesses the Scriptures as a type of the sacred books generally. That must in each case be said *first* by liberalism, before it makes the distinction of "higher" and "lower" among these many options.

The confusion of thought in our times is furthered by the failure of numbers of chastened and revitalized liberal scholars, to make clear that it is necessary for them, while they stand in the liberal framework, to conform their more recent pronouncements about the uniqueness of Christianity, of regeneration, of the incarnation, of the Scriptures, to the dogma of continuity, of extreme divine immanence, of anti-miracle, which makes impossible any once-for-all, essentially unique, qualitatively distinct religion, religious experience, religious incarnation, religious literature. This necessity must not be obscured, from the liberal perspective, of fitting Christianity into the context of the world religions, regeneration into a framework of varieties of religious experience, Jesus Christ into the company of the supreme religious figures of all faiths, the Bible into a setting of the great religious classics.

So too, evangelical theology can be true to its own genius only by a denial of the liberal affirmation at this very central point, that is, by its assertion of the essential uniqueness of Christianity among the world religions as alone a redemptive religion in the proper sense, of Christian experience as alone a "saving" experience, of Christ Jesus as alone the Word of God incarnate, and of the Scriptures as alone the Word of God written. That must in all cases be said *first* by a conservative theologian, before he speaks of the relation of Christianity and the non-Christian religions, of Christian conversion and religious experience elsewhere, of this Christ and Bible and other "Christs" and "Bibles" so-called.

It is not forbidden to conservative Protestantism to find a significance in the religious stream divorced from the Hebrew-Christian revelation, any more than it is forbidden to the liberal Protestant to find a difference in kind between Christianity and other religious. The misrepresentation of positions in this regard has issued from emotional antipathies rather than from critical thought. The modernist who asserts that the fundamentalist sees no significance in the non-Biblical religions is as wrong as the fundamentalist who declares that the modernist sees no significance in Christianity. The fact is that each side finds a significance, but yet a remarkably different significance, in both Christianity and the non-Biblical movements of faith. Therefore, in the interest of clarity, it is necessary to formulate this significance against the background of what each side is saying *first* and which, if either conceals or refuses to say, it ends its claim to be a distinctive and representative view.

That it is not forbidden Liberalism, if it wishes, to find in the Christian scheme of things the "highest type" of religious view, experience, achievement, literature, is clear from the apologetics of Liberalism itself. The missionary message of Liberalism, as against Humanism, has involved, insofar as Liberalism has not itself disintegrated into Humanism, a rejection of the humanistic thesis that the Christian framework (whether one thinks of its view of God, or religious experience, or Jesus Christ, or Scriptures), is not entitled to any special distinction in the religious arena, and, instead, shows up rather disadvantageously alongside some of the other religions, and is in rather drastic need of revision at central points. Liberal literature throbs with an emphasis on the "superiority" of the Christian God over other gods, of Christian conversion over other conversions, of Christ Jesus over other religious geniuses, of the Bible over other religious records. It is certainly not because Liberalism did not champion the "supremacy" of Christianity that evangelical Protestantism rivals it.

But while Liberalism declared that the Christian scheme is "higher" than that of the movement of world religions generally, it was forbidden to Liberalism — in view of its basic dogma of "continuity" — to declare that Christianity, in whole or in part, is different "in kind," is qualitatively unique, in contrast with the other religions. Liberalism has not always made clear that this assertion that Christianity is "higher" was intended as a denial that it is qualitatively different. The proponents of Liberalism stressed that Christianity is so vastly superior to the other religions that the difference in degree "practically" comes to a difference in kind. They stressed that the psychology of Christian experience had something over and above to offer the psychology of Mohammedan or Buddhist experience. They emphasized the "relative absoluteness" of Christ and affirmed their personal faith that no higher incarnation of the divine than that in him would ever appear. They asserted the Scriptures to be different precisely because of the historical record which they afford of the beginnings of this distinctive movement. But all of this came in the end to a circuitous, and sometimes in the case of the so-called "heresy" trials, a very convenient, way of denying that Christianity is the only true religion, of denying that men without Christian rebirth could not see the kingdom of heaven, of denying that Christ Jesus is the only name under heaven given among men whereby they must be saved, of denying that the Bible is in an exclusive sense the Word of God written. That is to say, Liberalism's praises of Christianity and its content came in the course of repudiating what Christianity historically has asserted about itself.

Just as Liberalism felt driven to deny the qualitative uniqueness of Christianity and Christian experience, so Evangelism was driven to affirm that Christianity is the one true religion which alone contains the "saving" essence of religion, that without Christian regeneration men are outside the benefits of Christ's salvation, that Christ Jesus is a once-for-all Divine incarnation whose personality is resident on the side of His deity, that the Bible is the only book of its kind because it is the result of the Divine purpose to inscripturate God's special saving revelation to mankind.

Nor did this mean that evangelical Christianity simply closed its eyes to other religious phenomena, as if they do not exist. If liberal theologians assert that wherever men interact with the good, the true, the beautiful, be it in the most primitive or the most advanced spiritual movements, there men are engaged in genuine religious experience, conservative theologians say no less. It stands at the very heart of a Biblical view of things that men everywhere are related to God as sinners, and in emphasizing that men are sinners the evangelical theology emphasizes not that they are unrelated to God, but that they are related by way of revolt. That God is revealed in various degrees in the non-Christian religious movements is not concession made grudgingly by evangelical theology, but rather is an insistence which is necessary to the evangelical view of man's predicament in sin. God has not left Himself anywhere without a witness, and in relationship to whatever light there is in the non-Christian religions man is an estranged sinner walking at a distance from the Lord of heaven and earth.

But that is another thing from saying that Biblical and non-Biblical religion are cut from the same piece of cloth, so that one is merely a higher expression of the others. That is precisely what evangelical theology is driven not to say. If the non-Christian religions exhibit with more or less brokenness the claim of the righteous God upon the consciences of men — and the extent of the brokenness with which they do so is evident both from Paul's treatment of their declension in the first chapter of the epistle to the Romans and from any empirical survey of the range of religious perspectives abroad in the world today — the Hebrew-Christian revelation, and it alone, enters as a special incursion into this pattern of religiosity and offers salvation in a sense which is unknown in the stream of general religions. That God is holier than men think, so holy indeed that men cannot save themselves by the effort of human works; that

God is more loving than men think, so loving indeed that He offers to provide on the condition of repentance and faith a salvation which it is not in man's power to attain; that the God of holy love provides salvation not by cancelling the debt of sin as if it really does not matter, but rather provides it by a substutionary atonement in and through the Mediator — these central emphases of Biblical revelation are not to be absorbed to the other religions as exhibiting more clearly something which they teach in a more elemental way, but rather as the direct negation of the way of "salvation" so far as they lead on clearly to the implications of a personal and ethical Deity. Salvation by works is not an elementary version of salvation by faith alone in the substitutionary death of the Mediator, but rather its very negation, as Christianity has had in turn to remind even post-Christian Judaism and Roman Catholicism. And that is precisely why evangelical theology has been careful to insist that the "saving" essence of religion is to be found in Hebrew-Christian revelation, and nowhere else, and that any effort to represent Biblical Christianity as the "highest" expression of what is found in the non-Christian religions either misunderstands them or misunderstands Christianity.

The twentieth century theological scene witnessed the rise of what is called Fundamentalism. As against Modernism, which in some of its emphases was as ancient as pre-Christian paganism, it stood in central continuity with Biblical Christianity. But since it was in a sense reactionary, that is, since its basic position was formulated with Modernism as much as Biblical theology on the horizon of its thought, it was sometimes drawn into saying *first* what an evangelical needs to say, but without the complete perspective in which it needs to be said, that is, without saying also what equally well, if not more properly, needs to be said first. What fundamentalists frequently said first was the virgin birth of Jesus Christ, His physical resurrection, His physical return, the eternal punishment of unbelievers — elements of Biblical Christianity which served strategically as direct tests of an individual's continuance within the historic faith, since it was difficult for modernists in these connections to employ that ambiguous vocabulary which could make a difference of degree appear like a difference of kind. But the continued fundamentalist emphasis on such isolated doctrinal elements, without an equally emphatic emphasis on what needed quite as much to be said in view of the basic modernistic assumptions, gave the main stream of evangelical Protestantism a certain reactionary overcast during the past generation. It cannot be gainsaid that, in its firm stand for the Deity of Christ, His virgin birth and sinless life, substitutionary atonement and bodily resurrection, high priestly ministry and second advent, and equally for the high view of the Bible as God's inscripturated revelation, Fundamentalism maintained against Modernism the most vigorous presentation of supernaturalistic Christianity to be found on the recent theological scene in America. But that is no reason for minimizing that something in the way of apologetic acumen and strategy was often missing from its case for Biblical theism.

But Fundamentalism was not alone in being "maneuvered" into saying something in a characteristic way. Modernism too had a way of setting up the traditional theology in terms of certain straw images: a deity who produced man by fiat creation "obviously" belonged to the realm of the myths; an esentially divine Christ "obviously" could not possess a human nature; the central Biblical concern "obviously" was not individual redemption but social justice; one who believed in original sin and in miracle "obviously" was an obscurantist.

The only thing that was conspicuously obvious about all of this, it becomes increasingly apparent, was the frame of reference which "compelled" Liberalism to say first what it feels it is driven to say first. The dogma of continuity was the reason why it was and is *verboten* for Liberalism to say first what evangelical Protestantism is driven to say first. This dogma of an unrelieved continuity of history so ties together all events within one seamless net that no exceptions are to be made, not even for the Hebrew-Christian tradition in all or in part. And from what is the "compulsion" of the dogma of continuity derived? Certainly not from empirical observation, that much can be said without fear of contradiction. True, the modernist might reply and say that the experience of the last century, in which the detailed observation of the behavior of nature and history has been especially prosecuted, has disclosed nothing but an all-embracing continuity. The reply is that, even if this were so, nobody has a right in the name of *science* to declare (as Modernism did, in the interest of so-called "scientific" theology), on the basis of the observation of nature and history over a period of one-hundred years, in limited places and limited times, what nature must be like in all places and times. For it is precisely a scientific view which is not entitled to legislate in advance, and for that matter, is not entitled to legislate in retrospect, as to what nature must be and must have been like, except as it has actually observed that behavior. The observation by scientists, if such observation there has really been, of an uncompromised continuity in nature at present is compatible either with an uncompromised continuity in all times, or with a compromised continuity at some times, and the issue is not settled by what the scientist observes in the present. If a pronouncement is made that nature *must always* have been or *must always* be totally uniform, it is precisely by the abandonment of a scientific attitude, and the substitution of a philosophic attitude — and moreover a philosophic attitude which is taken despite the inability of scientific observation to determine the issue one way or the other, and hence a non-scientific philosophic attitude — that this is ventured. But the fact of the matter is that, during the very years that liberal theology insisted that the scientifically-buttressed continuity of nature compelled it to say first what it said first, in competition with evangelical theology, able scientists, who were engaged in scientific studies and not in theological reconstruction, were denying that the observations of nature "demanded" a declaration of a total causal continuity. Max Planck's quantum theory in physics, and Heisenberg's principle of indeterminacy, are dated closer to the beginning of our century than to its mid-point, and both views involved a generous emphasis on the inability of the scientist, in terms of actual observation, to explain nature by a reductionistic causal continuity.[1] Consequently, the claim of Liberalism, that

---

1. Cf. the writer's *Remaking the Modern Mind*, especially the chapters on "The Continuity of Nature." The point at issue above is simply the extent to which liberal theology, professedly empirical, was actually so, and not whether the case for miracle is to be defended in terms of the presence of discontinuities in nature as we observe it. The author is far from ready to concede the liberal bias that the empirical sciences are to legislate in advance what the nature of Christianity as a theological science must be.

the claim to Hebrew-Christian revelation could not be allowed in terms of a modern scientific view of the universe, is shown to be profoundly unscientific, for contemporary scientists could hardly claim to have observed the connections of all events, and indeed some of them were insisting that a complete causal uniformity was not perceptible to the senses in some events which they were observing in the immediate present.

The liberal dogma of continuity, actually, gained its force from certain modern philosophies more than from modern science; it was in the name of these philosophies, and not in the name of scientific observation, that it was "necessary" for Liberalism first to say what it did. Those philosophies are associated primarily with the names of Hegel and Darwin. In distinctive ways, they are evolutionary philosophies, their common point being an emphasis on extreme divine immanence. It is unnecessary here to develop those philosophies in detail; what is relevantly necessary is a clear indication of how this view of a radical divine immanence became the womb out of which the liberal dogma of continuity issued. Hegel's philosophy was a pantheistic idealism: nature and man are identical with God, are, indeed, God's self-externalization by a process of logical evolution. A philosophy in which all events are in the same sense the direct activity of the Absolute makes impossible the distinguishing of certain events in which the Absolute is peculiarly revealed, in contrast with other events. Hence Hegelian speculation worked itself out in direct hostility to the Biblical emphasis on a special, once-for-all miraculous manifestation of the Divine, since it allowed only a universe in which all events are similarly supernatural. Darwin's philosophy sought more of a scientific, less of a speculative base, but at the central point of the nature of the divine immanence it worked itself into an antipathy toward Biblical theology no less rigid than that of Hegelianism. The central feature of Darwin's view was that evolution is God's method of working, i. e., God works only by the production of complex effects from more simple causes through gradual, almost imperceptible change. Although the Darwinian view was not necessarily pantheistic, yet at the crucial point of God's relation to man and nature any significance of God as transcendent was eliminated, so that this philosophy struck as vigorously against Biblical supernaturalism as had the Hegelian view; the emphasis on slow and graded change ruled out all miracle, all irruption, all discontinuity.

It is not the task of this study to show how unphilosophical Hegelian pantheistic evolutionism is, nor how unscientific Darwin biological evolutionism is, although it doubtless should be mentioned that subsequent philosophy and science have had somewhat to say on this score. Hegelian pantheism did violence to the moral nature of the universe, and Darwinian evolutionism did violence to physical nature. As to absolutistic idealism of the Hegelian variety, it has very few influential exponents today; even the idealistic traditions which carry forward Hegel's absorption of nature and man to God do so in such a way, as for example in Personalism, as to place selves outside of God, in order to maintain significance for moral freedom and responsibility. As to Darwinian evolutionism, its emphasis that all living species have been produced by slow change from less complex forms has been so contradicted by the enterprise of paleontology, which instead of exhibiting everywhere biological forms in transition, as one would expect if the Darwinian hypothesis were true, exhibits instead the relative constancy of species in all periods, that for more than a generation the evolutionary hypothesis has been in process of reconstruction in the interest of an emergent theory, in which the appearance of novel species is anything but gradual and almost imperceptible.

Although the revolt against Hegel and Darwin has involved, therefore, a modification of the doctrine of extreme divine immanence in the sense in which those thinkers urged it, Liberalism in its classic expression, supposedly in the interests of a scientific theology, continued to oppose the essential uniqueness of Christianity, Biblical regeneration, Jesus Christ, and the Scriptures, on the basis of a dogma of continuity which could only be derived from the radical doctrine of immanence which everywhere else was breaking down. For a half generation now, especially under the pressure of the sociological turn of events, this emphasis on exaggerated immanence has been increasingly compromised, until in America a whole school of "realistic theologians" has come to the fore which, with regard to morality, urges the divine transcendence in such a way as to stress the sinfulness of man, without likewise relating the divine transcendence to nature in such a manner as to reintroduce the Biblical miraculous and special revelation. Hence it is necessary to emphasize that the transition from a liberal to an evangelical theology is not made in terms merely of an emphasis, in some manner or other, on the divine transcendence as well as immanence; there have been times in the history of philosophy when Biblical theology has had its rival in a non-Biblical formulation of divine transcendence, no less than of divine immanence. The turning point to an evangelical theology comes when one recognizes the neces-

sity of saying *first* what Liberalism has never permitted itself to say first, and what Evangelism is compelled to say
first: that Christianity, and Christian experience, and the
divine incarnation in Christ, and the sacred Scriptures, are
not simply a higher variation of a general principle exhibited
elsewhere, but belong to the distinctively soteriological movement of God, who has here done what He has done in grace,
what He has done nowhere else, so that they are qualitatively
distinct, and constitute the lone hope for man lost in the
darkness of sin.

If we have inquired into the necessity which Liberalism
feels for its denials at this point, it is important also to in-
quire into the compulsion for the assertions which Evangeli-
calism makes. And this inquiry is not one which Evangeli-
calism views with reluctance; rather, it welcomes and even
urges investigation of this kind. Liberalism has been all
too prone to assume smugly that there is nothing to investi-
gate; since it was precommitted to absolute uniformity, what
could the Hebrew-Christian claim be but unscientific superstition?

Everything else but, the evangelical replies. The evangelical compulsion to view Christianity, and its Founder, and
redemption, and the Bible, in this special way, derives not
from a philosophy of nature, but from *the living God who
has spoken, who has inscripturated His revelation, and enters into personal relations with men*. That is to say, the
necessity for asserting the qualitative distinctness of the
Hebrew-Christian revelation grows out of the nature of that
revelation itself, out of what God says here and says nowhere else, and out of how He says it here and says it nowhere else. That is the way Biblical revelation has always

understood itself, and this understanding grows not out of a peculiarity of the Hebrew-Christian community, but out of a peculiarity of the divine revelation which is addressed to it, and with which the Bible confronts us.

Biblical revelation is soteriological revelation, is the revelation which the merciful God gives to sinful man in revolt against Him. It is here and here alone that God declares the majesty of His holiness over against the awfulness of man's sin, it is here and here alone that He declares that there is no way from sinful man to the holy Lord, it is here and here alone that He declares that the just and loving God Himself provides a way, it is here and here alone that in promise and fulfillment the name of Jesus Christ is known, it is here and here alone that the special, saving revelation of God is communicated. And it is out of this necessity, in the experience of maturing to the intrinsic nature of the Hebrew-Christian revelation, that the evangelical Protestant affirmation of Biblical revelation and its concommitants, flows — not out of a necessity which seems to flow, but really does not, from modern science, nor out of a necessity which flows, as indeed it does not, out of the requirements of a pure philosophy, but rather out of the requirements which special revelation itself places upon those who hear the voice of God here.

The alternatives, therefore, have been radically misunderstood by Liberalism, and that is why it could only be a transition phenomenon in the sphere of theology. For the alternate of Biblical revelation understood as a once-for-all soteriological revelation of God has never been, on any direct reading of the evidence, Biblical revelation understood as the highest expression of what is everywhere else anticipated; the latter is necessarily a profound misunderstanding against which the Biblical revelation itself protests on any fair and objective reading. The real alternative to Biblical revelation as qualitatively unique is the denial of Biblical revelation; the real opposition to Hebrew-Christian revelation is a Liberalism from which the enduring significance of Jesus Christ is forever eliminated; the real antagonist of Biblical revelation is not mythology as Liberalism wrote mythology, but rather a mythology which knows only gods who never speak and act, gods who say and do only what men say, gods which are structures of men's minds and hands to serve their sinful purposes in rebellion against the one true God. The alternatives consistently reduce, in our day as in any, to Biblical theology or naturalistic nihilism.

INDEX

Index of Persons

DATE DUE

DEC 1 0 1993			
APR 2 4 1995			